Perfect Chicken Dinners

The Family Food Collection

D1644536

First published in 2012
LOVE FOOD is an imprint of Parragon Books Ltd

Parragon
Queen Street House
4 Queen Street
Bath BA1 1HE, UK

www.parragon.com

ISBN: 978-1-4454-7904-0

Printed in China

Produced by Ivy Contract
Photography by Charlie Paul

Notes for the Reader

This book uses both metric and imperial measurements. Follow the same units of measurement throughout; do not mix metric and imperial. All spoon measurements are level: teaspoons are assumed to be 5 ml, and tablespoons are assumed to be 15 ml. Unless otherwise stated, milk is assumed to be full fat, eggs and individual vegetables are medium, and pepper is freshly ground black pepper.

The times given are an approximate guide only. Preparation times differ according to the techniques used by different people and the cooking times may also vary from those given. Optional ingredients, variations or serving suggestions have not been included in the calculations.

Recipes using raw or very lightly cooked eggs should be avoided by infants, the elderly, pregnant women, convalescents and anyone suffering from an illness. Pregnant and breastfeeding women are advised to avoid eating peanuts and peanut products. Sufferers from nut allergies should be aware that some of the ready-made ingredients used in the recipes in this book may contain nuts. Always check the packaging before use.

Perfect Chicken Dinners

introduction

Chicken has become one of the most useful and popular meats in nearly all cultures around the world. The reasons for this are many, not least that chickens are relatively quick and easy to raise, and do not require acres of lush grassland! It is worth bearing in mind that a free-range, corn-fed chicken might cost a little more, but it will have a far superior flavour to one that has been intensively farmed.

From a nutritional point of view, chicken is an excellent source of protein, B vitamins and minerals such as zinc and iron. It is naturally low in fat and has no carbohydrates, making it the dream food for those who need to keep their weight or cholesterol levels in check. It is very quick and easy to cook, too, so there need be no excuses about not having enough time to produce a healthy, well-balanced meal!

And from a gastronomic point of view? There are so many options that you could serve chicken every day of the week and still not run out of ideas! Chicken can be cooked very simply – roasted, chargrilled, grilled, stir-fried or pan-fried – and served with potatoes or rice and salad leaves or lightly cooked vegetables. And when you have a little more time to spare, the choices are endless. If you like rice, you can go for a creamy Italian risotto or a saffron-coloured Spanish paella; and if you are a pasta lover, you will find some fantastic sauces and might even be inspired to make your own filled pasta shapes, such as tortellini and ravioli. If Mexican food is your thing, there are traditional recipes to suit you; and there are Chinese, Thai and Indian dishes to satisfy spice cravings!

Whatever your choice, you will enjoy the flavour and variety that these recipes have to offer.

soups, starters & salads

cream of chicken soup

ingredients

serves 4

3 tbsp butter

4 shallots, chopped

1 leek, sliced

450 g/1 lb skinless chicken
   breasts, chopped

600 ml/1 pint chicken stock

1 tbsp chopped fresh parsley

1 tbsp chopped fresh thyme,
   plus extra sprigs to garnish

175 ml/6 fl oz double cream

salt and pepper

method

1 Melt the butter in a saucepan over a medium heat. Add the shallots and cook, stirring, for 3 minutes, until softened. Add the leek and cook for a further 5 minutes, stirring. Add the chicken, stock and herbs, and season. Bring to the boil, then simmer for 25 minutes, until the chicken is cooked through. Remove from the heat and leave to cool for 10 minutes.

2 Transfer the soup to a food processor or blender and process until smooth (you may need to do this in batches). Return the soup to the rinsed-out pan and warm over a low heat for 5 minutes.

3 Stir in the cream and cook for a further 2 minutes, then remove from the heat and ladle into serving bowls. Garnish with sprigs of thyme and serve immediately.

variation

For a low fat option, omit the double cream and replace half the chicken stock with semi-skimmed milk. The soup will still taste smooth and creamy.

chicken & potato soup with bacon

ingredients

serves 4

1 tbsp butter
2 garlic cloves, chopped
1 onion, sliced
250 g/9 oz smoked lean back
    bacon, chopped
2 large leeks, sliced
2 tbsp plain flour
1 litre/1¾ pints chicken stock
800 g/1 lb 12 oz potatoes,
    chopped
200 g/7 oz skinless chicken
    breast, chopped
4 tbsp double cream
salt and pepper
grilled bacon and sprigs of fresh
    flat-leaf parsley, to garnish

method

1 Melt the butter in a large saucepan over a medium heat. Add the garlic and onion and cook, stirring, for 3 minutes, until slightly softened. Add the chopped bacon and leeks and cook for a further 3 minutes, stirring continuously.

2 In a bowl, mix the flour with enough stock to make a smooth paste, then stir it into the pan. Cook, stirring, for 2 minutes. Pour in the remaining stock, then add the potatoes and chicken. Season with salt and pepper. Bring to the boil, then lower the heat and simmer for 25 minutes, until the chicken and potatoes are tender and cooked through.

3 Stir in the cream and cook for a further 2 minutes, then remove from the heat and ladle into serving bowls. Garnish with the grilled bacon and flat-leaf parsley, and serve immediately.

chicken & broccoli soup

ingredients

serves 4–6

225 g/8 oz head broccoli
55 g/2 oz unsalted butter
1 onion, chopped
225 g/8 oz basmati rice
225 g/8 oz skinless, boneless
    chicken breast, cut into
    thin slivers
25 g/1 oz plain wholewheat flour
300 ml/10 fl oz milk
500 ml/16 fl oz chicken stock
55 g/2 oz sweetcorn kernels
salt and pepper

method

1 Break the broccoli into small florets and cook in a saucepan of lightly salted boiling water for 3 minutes, drain, then plunge into cold water and set aside.

2 Melt the butter in a pan over medium heat, add the onion, rice and chicken, and cook for 5 minutes, stirring frequently.

3 Remove the pan from the heat and stir in the flour. Return to the heat and cook for 2 minutes, stirring constantly. Stir in the milk and then the stock. Bring to the boil, stirring constantly, then reduce the heat and simmer for 10 minutes.

4 Drain the broccoli and add to the pan with the sweetcorn and salt and pepper. Simmer for a further 5 minutes, or until the rice is tender, then serve.

thai chicken-coconut soup

ingredients

serves 4

115 g/4 oz dried vermicelli noodles
1.2 litres/2 pints chicken or
    vegetable stock
1 lemon grass stalk, crushed
1-cm/½-inch piece fresh ginger,
    peeled and very finely chopped
2 fresh kaffir lime leaves,
    thinly sliced
1 fresh red chilli, or to taste,
    deseeded and thinly sliced
2 skinless, boneless chicken
    breasts, thinly sliced
200 ml/7 fl oz coconut cream
2–3 tbsp Thai fish sauce
1–2 tbsp fresh lime juice
55 g/2 oz beansprouts
4 spring onions, green part only,
    finely sliced
fresh coriander leaves, to garnish

method

1 Soak the dried noodles in a large bowl with enough lukewarm water to cover for 20 minutes, until soft. Or, cook according to the packet instructions. Drain well and set aside.

2 Meanwhile, bring the stock to the boil in a large saucepan over a high heat. Lower the heat, add the lemon grass, ginger, lime leaves and chilli and simmer gently for 5 minutes. Add the chicken and continue simmering for a further 3 minutes, or until cooked.

3 Stir in the coconut cream, Thai fish sauce and 1 tablespoon of lime juice and continue simmering for 3 minutes. Add the beansprouts and spring onions and simmer for a further 1 minute.

4 Taste and gradually add extra fish sauce or lime juice, if needed. Remove and discard the lemon grass stalk.

5 Divide the vermicelli noodles between 4 bowls. Bring the soup back to the boil, then add to each bowl. The heat of the soup will warm the noodles. To garnish, sprinkle with coriander leaves.

chicken & tarragon soup

ingredients

serves 4

55 g/2 oz unsalted butter
1 large onion, chopped
300 g/10½ oz cooked skinless
 chicken, shredded finely
625 ml/1 pint chicken stock
1 tbsp chopped fresh tarragon
150 ml/5 fl oz double cream
salt and pepper
fresh tarragon leaves, to garnish
deep-fried crôutons, to serve

method

1 Melt the butter in a large saucepan and fry the onion for 3 minutes.

2 Add the chicken to the pan with half of the chicken stock. Bring to the boil, then reduce the heat and simmer for 20 minutes. Let cool, then process until smooth in a blender or food processor.

3 Return the soup to the pan to heat through. Add the remainder of the stock to the mixture and season with salt and pepper. Add the chopped tarragon, then transfer the soup to individual serving bowls and stir in the cream.

4 Garnish the soup with fresh tarragon and serve with deep-fried crôutons.

clear soup with mushrooms & chicken

ingredients

serves 4

25 g/1 oz dried ceps or other
    mushrooms
1 litre/1¾ pints water
2 tbsp vegetable or peanut oil
115 g/4 oz mushrooms, sliced
2 garlic cloves, chopped coarsely
5-cm/2-inch piece fresh galangal,
    sliced thinly
2 chicken breast portions
    (on the bone, skin on)
225 g/8 oz baby chestnut or white
    mushrooms, cut into quarters
juice of ½ lime
sprigs fresh flat-leaf parsley,
    to garnish

method

1 Place the dried mushrooms in a small bowl and pour over hot water to cover. Set aside to soak for 20–30 minutes. Drain the mushrooms, reserving the soaking liquid. Cut off the stalks and chop the caps coarsely.

2 Pour the reserved soaking water into a saucepan with the measured water and bring to the boil. Reduce the heat to a simmer.

3 Meanwhile, heat the oil in a wok and stir-fry the soaked mushrooms, sliced fresh mushrooms, garlic and galangal for 3–4 minutes. Add to the pan of hot water with the chicken breasts. Simmer for 10–15 minutes, until the meat comes off the bones easily.

4 Remove the chicken from the pan. Peel off and set aside the skin. Remove the meat from the bones, slice and set aside. Return the skin and bones to the stock and simmer for a further 30 minutes.

5 Remove the pan from the heat and strain the stock into a clean pan through a sieve lined with cheesecloth. Bring back to the boil and add the chestnut or white mushrooms, sliced chicken and lime juice. Reduce the heat and simmer for 8-10 minutes. Ladle into bowls, garnish with parsley sprigs and serve immediately.

chicken crostini

ingredients

serves 4

12 slices French bread
or country bread
4 tbsp olive oil
2 garlic cloves, chopped
2 tbsp finely chopped fresh
oregano
100 g/3¹/₂ oz cold roast chicken,
cut into small, thin slices
4 tomatoes, sliced
12 thin slices of goat's cheese
12 black olives, pitted and chopped
salt and pepper
fresh red and green salad leaves,
to serve

method

1 Put the bread under a preheated medium grill and lightly toast on both sides. Meanwhile, pour the olive oil into a bowl and add the garlic and oregano. Season with salt and pepper and mix well. Remove the toasted bread slices from the grill and brush them on one side only with the oil mixture.

2 Place the bread slices, oiled sides up, on a baking sheet. Put some sliced chicken on top of each one, followed by a slice of tomato.

3 Divide the slices of goat's cheese among the bread slices, then top with the chopped olives. Drizzle over the remaining oil mixture and transfer to a preheated oven, 180°C/350°F/Gas Mark 4. Bake for about 5 minutes, or until the cheese is golden brown and starting to melt.

4 Remove from the oven and serve with fresh red and green salad leaves.

chicken-noodle soup

ingredients

serves 4–6

2 skinless chicken breasts
2 litres/3½ pints water
1 onion, with skin left on,
    cut in half
1 large garlic clove, cut in half
1-cm/½-inch piece fresh ginger,
    peeled and sliced
4 black peppercorns, lightly
    crushed
4 cloves
2 star anise
1 carrot, peeled
1 celery stalk, chopped
100 g/3½ oz baby corn, cut in half
    lengthways and chopped
2 spring onions, finely shredded
115 g/4 oz dried rice vermicelli
    noodles
salt and pepper

method

1 Put the chicken breasts and water in a saucepan over
   high heat and bring to the boil. Reduce the heat to its
   lowest setting and simmer, skimming the surface until
   no more foam rises. Add the onion, garlic, ginger,
   peppercorns, cloves, star anise and a pinch of salt and
   continue to simmer for 20 minutes, or until the chicken
   is tender and cooked through. Meanwhile, grate the
   carrot along its length on the coarse side of a grater so
   you get long, thin strips.

2 Strain the chicken, reserving about 1.25 litres/2 pints
   stock, but discarding any flavouring ingredients.
   (At this point you can let the stock cool and refrigerate
   overnight, so any fat solidifies and can be lifted off and
   discarded.) Return the stock to the rinsed-out pan with
   the carrot, celery, baby corn and spring onions and
   bring to the boil. Boil until the baby corn are almost
   tender, then add the noodles and continue boiling for
   2 minutes.

3 Meanwhile, chop the chicken, add it to the pan and
   continue cooking for about 1 minute until the chicken
   is reheated and the noodles are soft. Add seasoning.

crispy chicken & ham croquettes

ingredients

makes 8

4 tbsp olive oil
4 tbsp plain flour
200 ml/7 fl oz milk
115 g/4 oz cooked chicken, ground
55 g/2 oz serrano or cooked ham,
    very finely chopped
1 tbsp chopped fresh flat-leaf
    parsley, plus extra sprigs
    to garnish
small pinch of freshly
    grated nutmeg
1 egg, beaten
55 g/2 oz day-old white
    breadcrumbs
corn oil, for deep-frying
salt and pepper
garlic mayonnaise, to serve

method

1 Heat the olive oil in a saucepan. Stir in the flour to form a paste and cook gently for 1 minute, stirring constantly. Gradually stir in the milk until smooth and slowly bring to the boil, stirring constantly, until the mixture boils and thickens.

2 Remove from the heat, add the ground chicken and beat until the mixture is smooth. Add the chopped ham, parsley and nutmeg and mix well together. Season with salt and pepper. Put in a dish and let stand for 30 minutes, until cool, then cover and let rest in the refrigerator for 2–3 hours or overnight.

3 Pour the beaten egg onto a plate and spread out the breadcrumbs on another plate. Divide the chilled chicken mixture into 8 portions, then shape to form cylindrical croquettes. Dip them, one at a time, in the beaten egg, then roll in the breadcrumbs to coat. Let chill in the refrigerator for 1 hour.

4 Heat the oil in a deep-fryer to 180–190°C/350–375°F. Add the croquettes, in batches to keep the temperature of the oil from dropping, and deep-fry for 5–10 minutes, or until golden brown and crispy. Remove with a slotted spoon and drain well on kitchen paper.

5 Serve the croquettes piping hot, garnished with parsley sprigs, with garlic mayonnaise.

chicken in lemon & garlic

ingredients

serves 6–8

4 large skinless, boneless chicken
  breasts
5 tbsp Spanish olive oil
1 onion, finely chopped
6 garlic cloves, finely chopped
grated rind of 1 lemon, finely pared
  rind of 1 lemon and juice
  of both lemons
4 tbsp chopped fresh flat-leaf
  parsley, plus extra to garnish
salt and pepper
lemon wedges and crusty bread
  (optional), to serve

method

1 Using a sharp knife, slice the chicken breasts widthways
  into very thin slices. Heat the olive oil in a large,
  heavy-based frying pan, add the onion and cook for
  5 minutes, or until softened, but not browned. Add
  the garlic and cook for a further 30 seconds.

2 Add the sliced chicken to the pan and cook gently for
  5–10 minutes, stirring from time to time, until all the
  ingredients are lightly browned and the chicken
  is tender.

3 Add the grated lemon rind and the lemon juice and
  let it bubble. At the same time, deglaze the pan by
  scraping and stirring all the bits on the bottom of the
  pan into the juices with a wooden spoon. Remove
  the skillet from the heat, stir in the parsley and season
  with salt and pepper.

4 Transfer, piping hot, to a warmed serving dish. Sprinkle
  with the pared lemon rind, garnish with the parsley
  and serve with lemon wedges for squeezing over the
  chicken, accompanied by chunks or slices of crusty
  bread, if using, for mopping up the juices.

soy chicken wings

ingredients

serves 3–4

250 g/9 oz chicken wings,
    defrosted if frozen
250 ml/8 fl oz water
1 tbsp sliced spring onion
2.5-cm/1-inch piece of fresh
    ginger, cut into 4 slices
2 tbsp light soy sauce
½ tsp dark soy sauce
1 star anise
1 tsp sugar

method

1 Wash and dry the chicken wings. In a small saucepan, bring the water to the boil, then add the chicken, spring onion and ginger and bring back to the boil.

2 Add the remaining ingredients, then cover and simmer for 30 minutes.

3 Using a slotted spoon, remove the chicken wings from any remaining liquid and serve hot.

chicken liver pâté

ingredients

serves 6–8

175 g/6 oz unsalted butter
500 g/1 lb 2 oz chicken livers,
    thawed if frozen, and trimmed
½ tbsp sunflower oil
2 shallots, finely chopped
2 large garlic cloves, finely
    chopped
2½ tbsp Madeira or brandy
2 tbsp double cream
1 tsp dried thyme
¼ tsp ground allspice
salt and pepper
toasted slices brioche and
    mixed salad leaves, to serve

method

1 Melt 25 g/1 oz of the butter in a large frying pan over medium–high heat. Add the chicken livers and stir for 5 minutes, or until they are brown on the outside, but still slightly pink in the centres. Work in batches, if necessary, to avoid overcrowding the pan.

2 Transfer the livers and their cooking juices to a food processor. Melt another 25 g/1 oz of the butter with the oil in the pan. Add the shallots and garlic and sauté, stirring frequently, for 2–3 minutes, until the shallots are soft, but not brown.

3 Add the Madeira and scrape up any cooking juices from the base. Stir in the cream, then the thyme, allspice, salt and pepper. Pour this mixture, with the cooking juices, into the food processor with the livers. Add the remaining butter, cut into small pieces.

4 Whiz the mixture in the food processor until smooth. Taste, and adjust the seasoning if necessary. Let the mixture cool slightly, then scrape into a serving bowl and set aside to allow the pâté to cool completely.

5 Serve immediately, or cover and store in the refrigerator for up to 3 days and let stand at room temperature for 30 minutes before serving. Serve with hot toasted brioche and mixed salad leaves.

mixed leaves with warm chicken livers

ingredients

serves 4

250 g/9 oz mixed salad leaves, torn into bite-size pieces
2 tbsp chopped fresh flat-leaf parsley
2 tbsp snipped fresh chives
3–4 tbsp olive oil
100 g/3½ oz shallots, finely chopped
1 large garlic clove, finely chopped
500 g/1 lb 2 oz chicken livers, cored, trimmed and halved
3 tbsp raspberry vinegar
salt and pepper
French bread, to serve (optional)

method

1 Toss the salad leaves with the parsley and chives and divide between individual plates.

2 Heat 2 tablespoons of the oil in a sauté pan or frying pan over medium–high heat. Add the shallots and garlic and sauté for 2 minutes, or until the shallots are soft, but not brown.

3 Add an extra tablespoon of the oil to the sauté pan and heat. Add the chicken livers and sauté for 5 minutes, or until they appear just pink in the centre when cut in half. Add a little extra oil to the pan while the chicken livers are sautéeing, if necessary.

4 Increase the heat to high, then add the raspberry vinegar and stir quickly. Season with salt and pepper, then spoon the livers and cooking juices over the mixed greens. Serve immediately with French bread, if using.

chicken, cheese & rocket salad

ingredients

serves 4

150 g/5½ oz rocket leaves
2 celery stalks, trimmed
    and sliced
½ cucumber, sliced
2 spring onions, trimmed
    and sliced
2 tbsp chopped fresh parsley
25 g/1 oz walnut pieces
350 g/12 oz boneless roast
    chicken, sliced
125 g/4½ oz Stilton cheese, cubed
handful of seedless red grapes,
    cut in half (optional)
salt and pepper

dressing

2 tbsp olive oil
1 tbsp sherry vinegar
1 tsp Dijon mustard
1 tbsp chopped
    mixed herbs

method

1 Wash the rocket leaves, pat dry with kitchen paper
   and put them into a large salad bowl. Add the celery,
   cucumber, spring onions, parsley and walnuts and mix
   together well. Transfer onto a large serving platter.
   Arrange the chicken slices over the salad, then scatter
   over the cheese. Add the red grapes, if using. Season
   well with salt and pepper.

2 To make the dressing, put all the ingredients into a
   screw-top jar and shake well. Alternatively, put them
   into a bowl and mix together well. Drizzle the dressing
   over the salad and serve.

roast chicken salad with orange dressing

ingredients

serves 4

250 g/9 oz young spinach leaves
handful of fresh parsley leaves
½ cucumber, thinly sliced
90 g/3¼ oz walnuts, toasted
    and chopped
350 g/12 oz boneless lean roast
    chicken, thinly sliced
2 red apples
1 tbsp lemon juice
fresh flat-leaf parsley sprigs,
    to garnish
orange wedges, to serve

orange dressing

2 tbsp extra-virgin olive oil
juice of 1 orange
finely grated rind
    of ½ orange
1 tbsp sour cream

method

1 Wash and drain the spinach and parsley leaves, if necessary, then arrange on a large serving platter. Top with the cucumber and walnuts. Arrange the chicken slices on top of the leaves.

2 Core the apples, then cut them in half. Cut each half into slices and brush with the lemon juice to prevent discoloration. Arrange the apple slices over the salad.

3 Place all the dressing ingredients in a screw-top jar, screw on the lid tightly and shake well until thoroughly combined. Drizzle the dressing over the salad, garnish with parsley sprigs and serve immediately with orange wedges.

chicken pinwheels with blue cheese & herbs

ingredients

serves 4

2 tbsp pine nuts, lightly toasted
2 tbsp chopped fresh parsley
2 tbsp chopped fresh thyme
1 garlic clove, chopped
1 tbsp grated lemon rind
4 large, skinless chicken breasts
250 g/9 oz blue cheese, such as
    Stilton, crumbled
salt and pepper
twists of lemon and sprigs of fresh
    parsley, to garnish
fresh green and red salad leaves,
    to serve

method

1 Put the pine nuts into a food processor with the parsley, thyme, garlic and lemon rind. Season with salt and pepper.

2 Pound the chicken breasts lightly to flatten them. Spread them on one side with the pine nut mixture, then top with the cheese. Roll them up from one short end to the other, so that the filling is enclosed. Wrap the rolls individually in foil and seal well. Transfer to a steamer, or a metal colander placed over a pan of boiling water, cover tightly and steam for 10–12 minutes, or until cooked through.

3 Arrange the salad leaves on a large serving platter. Remove the chicken from the heat, discard the foil, and cut the chicken rolls into slices. Arrange the slices over the salad leaves, garnish with twists of lemon and sprigs of parsley and serve.

cajun chicken salad

ingredients

serves 4

4 skinless, boneless chicken
    breasts, about 140 g/5 oz each
4 tsp Cajun seasoning
2 tsp corn oil (optional)
1 ripe mango, peeled, pitted and
    cut into thick slices
200 g/7 oz mixed salad leaves
1 red onion, thinly sliced and
    cut in half
175 g/6 oz cooked beetroot, diced
85 g/3 oz radishes, sliced
55 g/2 oz walnut halves
4 tbsp walnut oil
1–2 tsp Dijon mustard
1 tbsp lemon juice
salt and pepper
2 tbsp sesame seeds

method

1 Make 3 diagonal slashes across each chicken breast.
   Put the chicken into a shallow dish and sprinkle all
   over with the Cajun seasoning. Cover and chill for at
   least 30 minutes.

2 When ready to cook, brush a griddle pan with the
   corn oil, if using. Heat over high heat until very hot
   and a few drops of water sprinkled into the pan
   sizzle immediately. Add the chicken and cook for
   7–8 minutes on each side, or until thoroughly cooked.
   If still slightly pink in the centre, cook a little longer.
   Remove the chicken and set aside.

3 Add the mango slices to the pan and cook for
   2 minutes on each side. Remove from the pan and
   set aside.

4 Meanwhile, arrange the salad leaves in a salad bowl,
   reserving a few for a garnish, and sprinkle over the
   onion, beetroot, radishes and walnut halves.

5 Put the walnut oil, mustard, lemon juice, salt and
   pepper in a screw-top jar and shake until well blended.
   Pour over the salad and sprinkle with the sesame seeds.

6 Arrange the mango and the salad on a serving plate,
   top with the chicken breast and garnish with a few of
   the salad leaves.

gingered chicken & vegetable salad

ingredients

serves 4

4 skinless, boneless chicken breasts
4 spring onions, chopped
2.5-cm/1-inch piece ginger,
    chopped finely
2 garlic cloves, crushed
2 tbsp vegetable or peanut oil

salad

1 tbsp vegetable or peanut oil
1 onion, sliced
2 garlic cloves, chopped
115 g/4 oz baby corn, halved
115 g/4 oz mangetout, halved
    lengthways
1 red pepper, deseeded and sliced
7.5-cm/3-inch piece cucumber,
    peeled, deseeded and sliced
4 tbsp Thai soy sauce
1 tbsp jaggery or soft light
    brown sugar
few Thai basil leaves
175 g/6 oz fine egg noodles

method

1 Cut the chicken into large cubes, each about 2.5 cm/
1 inch. Mix the spring onions, ginger, garlic and oil
together in a shallow dish and add the chicken. Cover
and marinate for at least 3 hours. Lift the meat out of
the marinade and set aside.

2 To make the salad, heat the oil in a wok or large
frying pan and cook the onion for 1–2 minutes
before adding the rest of the vegetables, except the
cucumber. Cook for 2–3 minutes, until just tender.
Add the cucumber, half the soy sauce, the sugar and
the basil and mix gently.

3 Meanwhile, soak the noodles for 2–3 minutes (check
the packet instructions) or until tender and drain well.
Sprinkle the remaining soy sauce over them and
arrange on plates. Top with the cooked vegetables.

4 Add a little more oil to the wok, if necessary, and cook
the chicken over fairly high heat until browned on all
sides. Arrange the chicken cubes on top of the salad
and serve hot or warm.

red chicken salad

ingredients

serves 4

4 boneless chicken breasts
2 tbsp red curry paste
2 tbsp vegetable or peanut oil
1 head Napa cabbage, shredded
175 g/6 oz pak choi, torn into
   large pieces
½ savoy cabbage, shredded
2 shallots, chopped finely
2 garlic cloves, crushed
1 tbsp rice wine vinegar
2 tbsp sweet chilli sauce
2 tbsp Thai soy sauce

method

1 Slash the flesh of the chicken several times and rub the curry paste into each cut. Cover and chill overnight.

2 Cook in a heavy-based saucepan over medium heat or on a griddle pan for 5–6 minutes, turning once or twice, until cooked through. Keep warm.

3 Heat 1 tablespoon of the oil in a wok or large frying pan and stir-fry the Napa cabbage, pak choi and savoy cabbage until just wilted. Add the remaining oil, shallots and garlic and stir-fry until just tender, but not browned. Add the vinegar, chilli sauce and soy. Remove from the heat.

4 Arrange the leaves on 4 serving plates. Slice the chicken, arrange on the salad greens and drizzle the hot dressing over. Serve immediately.

thai chicken salad

ingredients

serves 6

vegetable oil spray
115 g/4 oz skinless chicken breast,
    cut lengthways horizontally
3 limes

dressing

1 tbsp finely shredded lemon grass
1 small green chilli, finely chopped
3 tbsp lime juice
1-cm/½-inch fresh ginger, peeled
    and thinly sliced into strips
1½ tsp sugar
2 tbsp white wine vinegar
3 fl oz water
1½ tsp cornflour

salad

25 g/1 oz rice vermicelli
50 g/1¾ oz peppers, deseeded
50 g/1¾ oz carrot
50 g/1¾ oz courgette
50 g/1¾ oz mangetout
50 g/1¾ oz baby corn
50 g/1¾ oz broccoli florets
50 g/1¾ oz pak choi
4 tbsp roughly chopped fresh
    coriander leaves

method

1 To make the dressing, put all the dressing ingredients, except the cornflour, into a small saucepan over low heat and bring to the boil. Blend the cornflour with a little cold water, gradually add to the pan, stirring constantly, and cook until thickened. Remove from the heat and leave to cool.

2 Heat a griddle pan over high heat and spray lightly with oil. Add the chicken and cook for 2 minutes on each side, or until thoroughly cooked through. Remove the chicken from the pan and shred.

3 To make the salad, cover the rice vermicelli with boiling water then let it cool in the water. Meanwhile, finely slice the peppers, carrot, courgette, mangetout and baby corn into strips. Cut the broccoli florets into 5-mm/¼-inch pieces and shred the pak choi. Drain the rice vermicelli and put all the salad ingredients with the chicken into a large bowl. Pour over the dressing and toss together, making sure that all the ingredients are well coated.

4 Cover and refrigerate for at least 2 hours before serving. Serve with the juice from half a lime squeezed over each portion.

lunch & light meals

spicy tomato chicken

ingredients

serves 4

500 g/1 lb 2 oz skinless, boneless
    chicken breasts
3 tbsp tomato purée
2 tbsp clear honey
2 tbsp Worcestershire sauce
1 tbsp chopped fresh rosemary
250 g/9 oz cherry tomatoes
fresh rosemary sprigs, to garnish
freshly cooked couscous or rice,
    to serve

method

1 Using a sharp knife, cut the chicken into 2.5-cm/1-inch
   chunks and place in a bowl. Mix the tomato purée,
   honey, Worcestershire sauce and rosemary together
   in a separate bowl, then add to the chicken, stirring
   to coat evenly.

2 Soak 8 wooden skewers in a bowl of cold water for
   30 minutes to prevent them burning during cooking.
   Preheat the grill to medium. Thread the chicken pieces
   and cherry tomatoes alternately onto the skewers and
   place them on a grill rack.

3 Spoon over any remaining glaze and cook under
   a preheated hot grill for 8–10 minutes, turning
   occasionally, until the chicken is cooked through.
   Transfer to 4 large serving plates, garnish with a few
   sprigs of fresh rosemary and serve with freshly cooked
   couscous or rice.

hot & spicy chicken with peanuts

ingredients

serves 4

marinade
2 tbsp soy sauce
1 tsp chilli powder (or to taste)

stir-fry
350 g/12 oz chicken breasts,
    skinned and cut into chunks
4 tbsp groundnut oil
1 clove garlic, finely chopped
1 tsp grated fresh ginger
3 shallots, thinly sliced
225 g/8 oz carrots, thinly sliced
1 tsp white wine vinegar
pinch of sugar
90 g/3¼ oz roasted peanuts
1 tbsp groundnut oil
cooked rice and coriander sprigs,
    to serve

method

1 To make the marinade, mix the soy sauce and chilli powder in a bowl. Add the chicken chunks and toss to coat. Cover with clingfilm and refrigerate for 30 minutes.

2 Heat the oil in a wok or frying pan, and stir-fry the chicken until browned and well cooked. Remove from the pan, set aside and keep warm.

3 If necessary, add a little more oil to the wok, then add the garlic, ginger, shallots and carrots. Stir-fry for 2–3 minutes.

4 Return the chicken to the wok and fry until it is warmed through. Add the vinegar, sugar and peanuts, stir well and drizzle with the groundnut oil.

5 Serve immediately with freshly cooked rice and coriander sprigs.

chicken satay

ingredients

serves 4

2 tbsp vegetable or peanut oil
1 tbsp sesame oil
juice of ½ lime
2 skinless, boneless chicken breasts,
    cut into small cubes

dip

2 tbsp vegetable or peanut oil
1 small onion, chopped finely
1 small fresh green chilli, deseeded
    and chopped
1 garlic clove, chopped finely
115 g/4 oz crunchy peanut butter
6–8 tbsp water
juice of ½ lime

method

1 Combine both the oils and the lime juice in a non-metallic dish. Add the chicken cubes, cover with clingfilm and chill for 1 hour. Soak 8–12 wooden skewers in cold water for 30 minutes before use, to prevent burning.

2 To make the dip, heat the oil in a frying pan and sauté the onion, chilli and garlic over low heat, stirring occasionally, for about 5 minutes, until just softened. Add the peanut butter, water and lime juice and simmer gently, stirring constantly, until the peanut butter has softened enough to make a dip – you may need to add a little extra water to make a thinner consistency.

3 Meanwhile, drain the chicken cubes and thread them onto the wooden skewers. Put under a hot grill or on a barbecue, turning frequently, for about 10 minutes, until cooked and browned. Serve the skewers hot with the warm dip.

five-spice chicken with vegetables

ingredients

serves 4

2 tbsp sesame oil
1 garlic clove, chopped
3 spring onions, trimmed
    and sliced
1 tbsp cornflour
2 tbsp rice wine
4 skinless chicken breasts,
    cut into strips
1 tbsp Chinese five-spice powder
1 tbsp grated fresh ginger
125 ml/4 fl oz chicken stock
100 g/3½ oz baby corn cobs, sliced
300 g/10½ oz beansprouts
finely chopped spring onions,
    to garnish, optional
freshly cooked jasmine rice,
    to serve

method

1 Heat the oil in a preheated wok or large frying pan. Add the garlic and spring onions and stir-fry over medium–high heat for 1 minute.

2 In a bowl, mix together the cornflour and rice wine, then add the mixture to the pan. Stir-fry for 1 minute, then add the chicken, five-spice powder, ginger and chicken stock and cook for another 4 minutes. Add the corn cobs and cook for 2 minutes, then add the beansprouts and cook for another minute.

3 Remove from the heat, garnish with chopped spring onions, if using, and serve with freshly cooked jasmine rice.

sweet-&-sour chicken

ingredients

serves 4–6

450 g/1 lb lean chicken meat,
    cubed
5 tbsp vegetable or peanut oil
1/2 tsp minced garlic
1/2 tsp finely chopped fresh ginger
1 green pepper, coarsely chopped
1 onion, coarsely chopped
1 carrot, finely sliced
1 tsp sesame oil
1 tbsp finely chopped spring onion
freshly cooked rice, to serve

marinade

2 tsp light soy sauce
1 tsp Shaoxing rice wine
pinch of white pepper
1/2 tsp salt
dash of sesame oil

sauce

8 tbsp rice vinegar
4 tbsp sugar
2 tsp light soy sauce
6 tbsp tomato ketchup

method

1 Place all the marinade ingredients in a bowl and
   marinate the chicken pieces for at least 20 minutes.

2 To prepare the sauce, heat the vinegar in a saucepan
   and add the sugar, light soy sauce and tomato
   ketchup. Stir to dissolve the sugar, then set aside.

3 In a preheated wok or deep pan, heat 3 tablespoons
   of the oil and stir-fry the chicken until it starts to turn
   golden brown. Remove and set aside.

4 In the clean wok or deep saucepan, heat the
   remaining oil and cook the garlic and ginger until
   fragrant. Add the vegetables and cook for 2 minutes.
   Add the chicken and cook for 1 minute. Finally add
   the sauce and sesame oil, then stir in the spring onion
   and serve with rice.

chicken with pak choi

ingredients

serves 4

175 g/6 oz broccoli
1 tbsp peanut oil
2.5-cm/1-inch piece fresh
    ginger, finely grated
1 fresh red Thai chilli, deseeded
    and chopped
2 garlic cloves, crushed
1 red onion, cut into wedges
450 g/1 lb skinless, boneless
    chicken breast, cut into
    thin strips
175 g/6 oz pak choi, shredded
115 g/4 oz baby corn, halved
1 tbsp light soy sauce
1 tbsp Thai fish sauce
1 tbsp chopped fresh coriander
1 tbsp toasted sesame seeds

method

1 Break the broccoli into small florets and cook in a saucepan of lightly salted boiling water for 3 minutes. Drain and set aside.

2 Heat a wok over high heat until almost smoking, add the oil, then add the ginger, chilli and garlic. Stir-fry for 1 minute. Add the onion and chicken and stir-fry for a further 3–4 minutes, or until the chicken is sealed on all sides.

3 Add the remaining vegetables to the wok, including the broccoli, and stir-fry the vegetables for 3–4 minutes, or until tender.

4 Add the soy and Thai fish sauces to the wok and stir-fry for a further 1–2 minutes, then serve at once, sprinkled with the coriander and sesame seeds.

creamy chicken curry with lemon rice

ingredients

serves 4

2 tbsp vegetable oil
4 skinless, boneless chicken
   breasts, 800 g/1 lb 12 oz
   in total, cut into 2.5-cm/1-inch
   pieces
1½ tsp cumin seeds
1 large onion, grated
2 fresh chillies, finely chopped
2 large garlic cloves, grated
1 tbsp grated fresh ginger
1 tsp ground turmeric
1 tsp ground coriander
1 tsp garam masala
300 ml/10 fl oz coconut milk
250 ml/9 fl oz canned tomatoes
2 tsp lemon juice
salt
2 tbsp chopped fresh coriander,
   to garnish

lemon rice

350 g/12 oz basmati rice, rinsed
1.25 litres/2 pints water
juice and grated rind of 1 lemon
3 cloves

method

1 Heat the oil in a large, heavy-based saucepan over
   medium heat. Add the chicken and cook for 5–8
   minutes, turning frequently, until lightly browned and
   cooked through. Remove from the pan and set aside.
   Add the cumin seeds and cook until they start to
   darken and sizzle. Stir in the onion, partially cover and
   cook over medium–low heat, stirring frequently, for
   10 minutes, or until soft and golden. Add the chillies,
   garlic, ginger, turmeric, ground coriander and garam
   masala and cook for 1 minute.

2 Return the chicken to the pan and stir in the coconut
   milk and the tomatoes. Partially cover and cook for
   15 minutes until the sauce has reduced and thickened.
   Stir in the lemon juice and season with salt.

3 Meanwhile, put the rice into a saucepan and cover
   with the water. Add the lemon juice and cloves. Bring
   to the boil, then reduce the heat, cover and simmer
   until the rice is tender and all the water has been
   absorbed. Remove the pan from the heat and stir in
   the lemon rind. Let the rice stand, covered, for 5 minutes.

4 Serve the curry with the lemon rice, sprinkled with
   fresh coriander.

thai green chicken curry

ingredients

serves 4

2 tbsp groundnut or sunflower oil
2 tbsp Thai green curry paste
500 g/1 lb 2 oz skinless, boneless
    chicken breasts, cut into cubes
2 kaffir lime leaves, roughly torn
1 lemon grass stalk, finely chopped
225 ml/8 fl oz coconut milk
16 baby aubergines, halved
2 tbsp Thai fish sauce
sprigs of fresh Thai basil and thinly
    sliced kaffir lime leaves,
    to garnish

method

1 Heat the oil in a preheated wok or large, heavy-based
  frying pan. Add the curry paste and stir-fry briefly until
  all the aromas are released.

2 Add the chicken, lime leaves and lemon grass and
  stir-fry for 3–4 minutes, until the meat is beginning
  to colour. Add the coconut milk and aubergines and
  simmer gently for 8–10 minutes, or until tender.

3 Stir in the fish sauce and serve immediately, garnished
  with sprigs of Thai basil and lime leaves.

variation

Replace the baby aubergines with 3 green peppers,
sliced, which will enhance the green colour of the curry.

chicken breasts with coconut milk

ingredients

serves 4

1 small onion, chopped

1 fresh green chilli, deseeded and chopped

2.5-cm/1-inch piece fresh ginger, chopped

2 tsp ground coriander

1 tsp ground cumin

1 tsp fennel seeds

1 tsp ground star anise

1 tsp cardamom seeds

½ tsp ground turmeric

½ tsp black peppercorns

½ tsp ground cloves

625 ml/1 pint canned coconut milk

4 skinless, boneless chicken breast portions

vegetable oil, for brushing

fresh coriander sprigs, to garnish

tomato rice and naan bread, to serve

method

1 Place the onion, chilli, ginger, coriander, cumin, fennel seeds, star anise, cardamom seeds, turmeric, peppercorns, cloves and 500 ml/16 fl oz of the coconut milk in a food processor and process to make a paste, adding more coconut milk if necessary.

2 Using a sharp knife, slash the chicken breasts several times and place in a large, shallow, non-metallic dish in a single layer. Pour over half the coconut milk mixture and turn to coat completely. Cover with clingfilm and marinate in the refrigerator for at least 1 hour, and up to 8 hours.

3 Heat a ridged griddle pan and brush lightly with vegetable oil. Add the chicken, in batches if necessary, and cook for 6–7 minutes on each side, or until tender.

4 Meanwhile, pour the remaining coconut milk mixture into a pan and bring to the boil, stirring occasionally. Arrange the chicken in a warmed serving dish, spoon over a little of the coconut sauce, and garnish with coriander sprigs. Serve hot with tomato rice and naan bread.

balti chicken

ingredients

serves 6

3 tbsp ghee or vegetable oil
2 large onions, sliced
3 tomatoes, sliced
1/2 tsp kalonji seeds
4 black peppercorns
2 cardamom pods
1 cinnamon stick
1 tsp chilli powder
1 tsp garam masala
1 tsp garlic purée
1 tsp ginger purée
salt
700 g/1 lb 9 oz skinless, boneless
    chicken breasts or thighs, diced
2 tbsp plain yogurt
2 tbsp chopped fresh coriander,
    plus extra to garnish
2 fresh green chillies, deseeded
    and finely chopped
2 tbsp lime juice
naan bread, to serve

method

1 Heat the ghee in a large, heavy-based frying pan.
   Add the onions and cook over low heat, stirring
   occasionally, for 10 minutes, or until golden. Add
   the sliced tomatoes, kalonji seeds, peppercorns,
   cardamoms, cinnamon stick, chilli powder, garam
   masala, garlic purée and ginger purée and season
   with salt. Cook, stirring constantly, for 5 minutes.

2 Add the chicken and cook, stirring constantly, for
   5 minutes, or until well coated in the spice paste. Stir
   in the yogurt. Cover and simmer, stirring occasionally,
   for 10 minutes.

3 Stir in the chopped coriander, chillies and lime juice.
   Transfer to a warmed serving dish, sprinkle with more
   chopped coriander and serve immediately with
   naan bread.

lime chicken with mint

ingredients

serves 6

3 tbsp finely chopped
    fresh mint
4 tbsp honey
4 tbsp lime juice
salt and pepper
12 boneless chicken thighs
mixed salad, to serve

sauce

150 ml/5 fl oz low-fat thick plain
    yogurt
1 tbsp finely chopped fresh mint
2 tsp finely grated lime rind

method

1 Mix the mint, honey and lime juice in a large bowl and
    season with salt and pepper. Use cocktail sticks to keep
    the chicken thighs in neat shapes and add the chicken
    to the marinade, turning to coat evenly.

2 Cover with clingfilm and marinate the chicken in the
    refrigerator for at least 30 minutes. Remove the chicken
    from the marinade and drain. Set aside the marinade.

3 Preheat the grill to medium. Place the chicken on
    a grill rack and cook under the hot grill for 15–18
    minutes, or until the chicken is tender and the juices
    run clear when the tip of a knife is inserted into the
    thickest part of the meat, turning the chicken
    frequently and basting with the marinade.

4 Meanwhile, combine all the sauce ingredients in a
    bowl. Remove the cocktail sticks and serve the chicken
    with a mixed salad and the sauce, for dipping.

bang bang chicken

ingredients

serves 4

350 g/12 oz boneless, skinless
   chicken meat
few drops of sesame oil
2 tbsp sesame paste
1 tbsp light soy sauce
1 tbsp chicken stock
½ tsp salt
pinch of sugar
8 tbsp shredded lettuce leaves
1 tbsp sesame seeds, roasted,
   to serve

method

1 Place the chicken in a saucepan of cold water, then
  bring to the boil and simmer for 8–10 minutes. Drain
  and let cool a little, then cut or tear the chicken into
  bite-size pieces.

2 Mix together the sesame oil, sesame paste, light soy
  sauce, chicken stock, salt and sugar and whisk until
  the sauce is thick and smooth. Toss in the chicken.

3 To serve, put the shredded lettuce on a large plate and
  spoon the chicken and sauce on top. Sprinkle with the
  sesame seeds and serve at room temperature.

thai spiced chicken with courgettes

ingredients

serves 4

1 tbsp olive oil

1 clove garlic, finely chopped

2.5-cm/1-inch piece fresh ginger, peeled and finely chopped

1 small fresh red chilli, deseeded and finely chopped

350 g/12 oz skinless, boneless chicken breasts, cut into thin strips

1 tbsp Thai 7-spice seasoning

1 red pepper and 1 yellow pepper, deseeded and sliced

2 courgettes, thinly sliced

227 g/8 oz canned bamboo shoots, drained

2 tbsp dry sherry or apple juice

1 tbsp light soy sauce

2 tbsp chopped fresh coriander, plus extra to garnish

salt and pepper

method

1 Heat the olive oil in a non-stick wok or large frying pan. Add the garlic, ginger and chilli and stir-fry for 30 seconds to release the flavours.

2 Add the chicken and Thai seasoning and stir-fry for about 4 minutes or until the chicken has coloured all over. Add the peppers and courgettes and stir-fry for 1–2 minutes or until slightly softened.

3 Stir in the bamboo shoots and stir-fry for a further 2–3 minutes or until the chicken is cooked through and tender. Add the sherry or apple juice, soy sauce and seasoning and sizzle for 1–2 minutes.

4 Stir in the chopped coriander and serve immediately, garnished with extra coriander.

bacon-wrapped chicken burgers

ingredients

serves 4

450 g/1 lb fresh ground chicken
1 onion, grated
2 garlic cloves, crushed
55 g/2 oz pine nuts, toasted
55 g/2 oz Gruyère cheese, grated
2 tbsp fresh snipped chives
2 tbsp wholewheat flour
8 lean back bacon rashers
1–2 tbsp corn oil
salt and pepper
mayonnaise and chopped spring
    onions (green part only),
    to garnish
crusty rolls, chopped lettuce and
    red onion rings, to serve

method

1 Place the ground chicken, onion, garlic, pine nuts, cheese, chives and salt and pepper in a food processor. Using the pulse button, blend the mixture together using short sharp bursts. Scrape out onto a board and shape into 4 even-size burgers. Coat in the flour, then cover and chill for 1 hour.

2 Wrap each burger with 2 bacon rashers, securing in place with a wooden cocktail stick.

3 Heat a heavy-based frying pan and add the oil. When hot, add the burgers and cook over medium heat for 5–6 minutes on each side, or until thoroughly cooked through.

4 Serve the burgers immediately in crusty rolls on a bed of lettuce and red onion rings and top with mayonnaise and spring onions.

chicken fajitas

ingredients

serves 4

3 tbsp olive oil, plus extra
    for drizzling
3 tbsp maple syrup or honey
1 tbsp red wine vinegar
2 garlic cloves, crushed
2 tsp dried oregano
1–2 tsp dried
    red pepper flakes
4 skinless, boneless chicken breasts
2 red peppers, deseeded and cut
    into 2.5-cm/1-inch strips
8 flour tortillas, warmed
salt and pepper
guacamole, to serve

method

1 Place the oil, maple syrup, vinegar, garlic, oregano,
  pepper flakes, salt and pepper in a large, shallow plate
  or bowl and mix together.

2 Slice the chicken across the grain into slices 2.5 cm/
  1 inch thick. Toss in the marinade until well coated.
  Cover and chill in the refrigerator for 2–3 hours, turning
  occasionally.

3 Heat a griddle pan until hot. Lift the chicken slices
  from the marinade with a slotted spoon, lay on the
  griddle pan and cook over medium–high heat for
  3–4 minutes on each side, or until cooked through.
  Remove the chicken to a warmed serving plate and
  keep warm.

4 Add the peppers, skin-side down, to the griddle pan
  and cook for 2 minutes on each side. Transfer to the
  serving plate.

5 Serve with the guacamole in the warmed tortillas.

chicken wraps

ingredients

serves 4

150 ml/5 fl oz low-fat plain yogurt
1 tbsp wholegrain mustard
280 g/10 oz cooked skinless,
    boneless chicken breast, diced
140 g/5 oz iceberg lettuce, finely
    shredded
85 g/3 oz cucumber, thinly sliced
2 celery stalks, sliced
85 g/3 oz black seedless grapes,
    halved
8 x 20-cm/8-inch soft flour
    tortillas or 4 x 25-cm/
    10-inch soft flour tortillas
pepper

method

1 Combine the yogurt and mustard in a bowl and season with pepper. Stir in the chicken and toss until thoroughly coated.

2 Put the lettuce, cucumber, celery and grapes into a separate bowl and mix well.

3 Fold a tortilla in half and in half again to make a cone that is easy to hold. Half-fill the tortilla pocket with the salad mixture and top with some of the chicken mixture. Repeat with the remaining tortillas, salad and chicken. Serve at once.

filo chicken pie

ingredients

serves 6–8

1.5 kg/3 lb 5 oz whole chicken
1 small onion, halved, and 3 large
    onions, chopped finely
1 carrot, sliced thickly
1 celery stalk, sliced thickly
pared rind of 1 lemon
1 bay leaf
10 peppercorns
155 g/5½ oz butter
55 g/2 oz plain flour
150 ml/5 fl oz milk
25 g/1 oz kefalotiri or romano
    cheese, grated
3 eggs, beaten
225 g/8 oz filo pastry (work with
    one sheet at a time and keep
    the remaining sheets covered
    with a damp tea towel)
salt and pepper

method

1 Put the chicken in a large saucepan with the halved onion, carrot, celery, lemon rind, bay leaf and peppercorns. Add water and bring to the boil. Cover and simmer for 1 hour, or until the chicken is cooked.

2 Remove the chicken and set aside to cool. Bring the stock to the boil and boil until reduced to about 625 ml/20 fl oz. Strain and reserve the stock. Cut the cooled chicken into pieces, without the skin and bones.

3 Fry the chopped onions until softened in 55 g/2 oz of the butter. Add the flour and cook gently, stirring, for 1–2 minutes. Gradually stir in the reserved stock and the milk. Bring to the boil, stirring constantly, then simmer for 1–2 minutes until thick and smooth. Remove from the heat, add the chicken and season. Leave to cool, then stir in the cheese and eggs.

4 Melt the remaining butter and use a little to grease a deep 30 x 20-cm/12 x 8-inch metal baking pan. Cut the pastry sheets in half widthways. Line the pan with one sheet of pastry and brush it with a little melted butter. Repeat with half of the pastry sheets. Spread the filling over the pastry, then top with the remaining pastry sheets, brushing each with butter and tucking down the edges. Bake in a preheated oven, 190°C/375°F/Gas Mark 5, for about 50 minutes, until golden. Serve warm.

pan-fried chicken & coriander

ingredients

serves 4

1 bunch of fresh coriander
1 tbsp corn oil
4 skinless, boneless chicken
    breasts, about 115 g/4 oz
    each, trimmed of all visible fat
1 tsp cornflour
1 tbsp water
90 ml/3 fl oz low-fat plain yogurt
2 tbsp reduced fat light cream
175 ml/6 fl oz chicken stock
2 tbsp lime juice
2 garlic cloves, finely chopped
1 shallot, finely chopped
1 tomato, peeled, deseeded
    and chopped
salt and pepper

method

1 Set aside a few coriander sprigs for a garnish and coarsely chop the remainder. Heat the corn oil in a heavy-based frying pan, add the chicken and cook over medium heat for 5 minutes on each side, or until the juices run clear when the meat is pierced with the tip of a sharp knife. Remove from the pan and keep warm.

2 Mix the cornflour and water until smooth. Stir in the yogurt and cream. Pour the chicken stock and lime juice into the frying pan and add the garlic and shallot. Reduce the heat and simmer for 1 minute. Stir the tomato into the yogurt mixture and stir the mixture into the pan. Season with salt and pepper. Cook, stirring constantly, for 1–2 minutes, or until slightly thickened, but do not let the mixture boil. Stir in the chopped fresh coriander.

3 Place the chicken on a large serving plate, pour the sauce over it and garnish with the reserved coriander sprigs. Serve.

chicken kebabs with yogurt sauce

ingredients

serves 4

300 ml/10 fl oz Greek-style yogurt
2 garlic cloves, crushed
juice of ½ lemon
1 tbsp chopped fresh herbs such
    as oregano, dill, tarragon
    or parsley
4 large skinned, boned chicken
    breasts
oil, for oiling
8 firm stems of fresh rosemary
    (optional)
salt and pepper
lemon wedges, to garnish
shredded romaine lettuce and rice,
    to serve

method

1 To make the sauce, put the yogurt, garlic, lemon juice, herbs, salt and pepper in a large bowl and mix well together.

2 Cut the chicken breasts into chunks measuring about 4 cm/1½ inches square. Add to the yogurt mixture and toss well together until the chicken pieces are coated. Cover and marinate in the refrigerator for about 1 hour. If you are using wooden skewers, soak them in cold water for 30 minutes before use.

3 Preheat the grill. Thread the pieces of chicken onto 8 flat, oiled, metal kebab skewers, wooden skewers or rosemary stems and place on an oiled griddle pan.

4 Cook the kebabs under the grill for about 15 minutes, turning and basting with the remaining marinade occasionally, until lightly browned and tender.

5 Pour the remaining marinade into a saucepan and heat gently but do not boil. Serve the kebabs with shredded lettuce on a bed of rice and garnish with lemon wedges. Accompany with the yogurt sauce.

gingered chicken kebabs

ingredients

serves 4

3 skinless, boneless chicken
breasts, cut into small cubes
juice of 1 lime
2.5-cm/1-inch piece fresh ginger,
peeled and chopped
1 fresh red chilli, deseeded
and sliced
2 tbsp vegetable or peanut oil
1 onion, sliced
2 garlic cloves, chopped
1 aubergine, cut into chunks
2 courgettes, cut into thick slices
1 red pepper, deseeded and cut
into squares
2 tbsp red curry paste
2 tbsp Thai soy sauce
1 tsp jaggery or soft light brown
sugar
boiled rice, with chopped
coriander, to serve

method

1 Put the chicken cubes in a shallow dish. Mix the lime,
ginger and chilli together and pour over the chicken
pieces. Stir gently to coat. Cover and chill in the
refrigerator for at least 3 hours to marinate.

2 Soak 8–12 wooden skewers in cold water for
30 minutes before use, to prevent burning.

3 Thread the chicken pieces onto the soaked wooden
skewers and cook under a hot grill for 3–4 minutes,
turning frequently, until they are cooked through.

4 Meanwhile, heat the oil in a wok or large frying pan
and sauté the onion and garlic for 1–2 minutes,
until softened, but not browned. Add the aubergine,
courgettes and pepper and cook for 3–4 minutes,
until cooked but still firm. Add the curry paste, soy
sauce and sugar and cook for 1 minute.

5 Serve hot with boiled rice, stirred through with
chopped coriander.

oriental glazed chicken wings

ingredients

serves 4

8 chicken wings, each wing
    chopped into 3 pieces
5 tbsp groundnut oil
6 tbsp chicken stock or water
2 tbsp chopped fresh coriander

marinade

1½ tbsp Shaoxing rice wine
    or dry sherry
1 tbsp soy sauce
1 tbsp rice vinegar
1½ tbsp sugar
¼ tsp salt
⅛ tsp Chinese five-spice seasoning
3 tbsp hoisin sauce
1 tsp finely chopped fresh ginger

method

1 To make the marinade, combine the wine, soy sauce
   and vinegar in a small bowl. Add the sugar, salt and
   five-spice seasoning, and stir until dissolved. Mix in
   the hoisin sauce and ginger.

2 Put the chopped chicken wings in a shallow dish
   and pour in the marinade, turning the wings to coat.
   Leave to marinate for 1 hour at room temperature,
   or overnight in the refrigerator.

3 Heat a wok over a high heat, add the oil and when it is
   almost smoking add the chicken wings and marinade.
   Stir-fry for 5 minutes, then sprinkle with 4 tablespoons
   of the stock and stir-fry for a further 4 minutes.

4 Using tongs, transfer the wings to a warmed serving
   dish, and sprinkle with the coriander. Pour off and
   discard most of the oil from the wok and return to the
   heat. Add the remaining 2 tablespoons of stock, and
   stir with a wooden spoon until blended, scraping up
   the sticky sediment. Pour into a small bowl and serve
   with the wings as a dipping sauce.

hearty dishes

traditional roast chicken

ingredients

serves 4

25 g/1 oz butter, softened
1 garlic clove,
    finely chopped
3 tbsp finely chopped
    toasted walnuts
1 tbsp chopped fresh parsley
salt and pepper
1 oven-ready chicken, weighing
    1.8 kg/4 lb
1 lime, cut into quarters
2 tbsp vegetable oil
1 tbsp cornflour
2 tbsp water
lime wedges and fresh rosemary
    sprigs, to garnish
roast potatoes and a selection
    of freshly cooked vegetables,
    to serve

method

1 Mix 1 tablespoon of the butter with the garlic, walnuts and parsley in a small bowl. Season well with salt and pepper. Loosen the skin from the breast of the chicken without breaking it. Spread the butter mixture evenly between the skin and breast meat. Place the lime quarters inside the body cavity.

2 Pour the oil into a roasting pan. Transfer the chicken to the pan and dot the skin with the remaining butter. Roast in a preheated oven, 190°C/375°F/Gas Mark 5, for 1¾ hours, basting occasionally, until the chicken is tender and the juices run clear when a skewer is inserted into the thickest part of the meat. Lift out the chicken and place on a serving platter to rest for 10 minutes.

3 Blend the cornflour with the water, then stir into the juices in the pan. Stir over low heat until thickened, adding more water if necessary. Garnish the chicken with lime wedges and rosemary sprigs. Serve with roast potatoes and a selection of freshly cooked vegetables and spoon over the thickened juices.

chicken & barley stew

ingredients

serves 4

2 tbsp vegetable oil
8 small, skinless chicken thighs
500 ml/18 fl oz chicken stock
100 g/3½ oz pearl barley, rinsed
    and drained
200 g/7 oz small new potatoes,
    scrubbed and halved
    lengthways
2 large carrots, peeled and sliced
1 leek, trimmed and sliced
2 shallots, sliced
1 tbsp tomato purée
1 bay leaf
1 courgette, trimmed and sliced
2 tbsp chopped fresh flat-leaf
    parsley, plus extra sprigs
    to garnish
2 tbsp plain flour
4 tbsp water
salt and pepper

method

1 Heat the oil in a large saucepan over a medium heat. Add the chicken and cook for 3 minutes, then turn over and cook on the other side for a further 2 minutes. Add the stock, barley, potatoes, carrots, leek, shallots, tomato purée and bay leaf. Bring to the boil, lower the heat and simmer for 30 minutes.

2 Add the courgette and chopped parsley, cover the pan and cook for a further 20 minutes, or until the chicken is cooked through. Remove the bay leaf and discard.

3 In a separate bowl, mix the flour with 4 tablespoons of water and stir into a smooth paste. Add it to the stew and cook, stirring, over a low heat for a further 5 minutes. Season to taste with salt and pepper.

4 Remove from the heat, ladle into individual serving bowls and garnish with sprigs of fresh parsley.

chicken, tomato & onion casserole

ingredients

serves 4

1½ tbsp unsalted butter
2 tbsp olive oil
1.8 kg/4 lb skinned chicken
    drumsticks
2 red onions, sliced
2 garlic cloves, finely chopped
400 g/14 oz canned chopped
    tomatoes
2 tbsp chopped flat-leaf parsley,
    plus extra to garnish
6 fresh basil leaves, torn
1 tbsp sun-dried tomato purée
150 ml/5 fl oz full-bodied red wine
225 g/8 oz mushrooms, sliced
salt and pepper

method

1 Heat the butter with the olive oil in a large ovenproof casserole. Add the chicken drumsticks and cook, turning frequently, for 5–10 minutes, or until golden all over and sealed. Using a slotted spoon, transfer the drumsticks to a plate.

2 Add the onions and garlic to the casserole and cook over low heat, stirring occasionally, for 10 minutes, or until golden. Add the tomatoes, the parsley, basil, tomato purée and wine, and season to taste with salt and pepper.

3 Bring to the boil, then return the chicken drumsticks to the casserole, pushing them down under the liquid. Cover and cook in a preheated oven, 160°C/325°F/Gas Mark 3, for 50 minutes.

4 Add the mushrooms and cook for a further 10 minutes, or until the chicken drumsticks are tender and the juices run clear when a skewer is inserted into the thickest part of the meat. Serve immediately, garnished with chopped parsley.

spiced chicken stew

ingredients

serves 6

1.8 kg/4 lb chicken pieces
2 tbsp paprika
2 tbsp olive oil
25 g/1 oz butter
450 g/1 lb onions, chopped
2 yellow peppers, deseeded
    and chopped
400 g/14 oz canned chopped
    tomatoes
225 ml/8 fl oz dry white wine
450 ml/16 fl oz chicken stock
1 tbsp Worcestershire sauce
½ tsp Tabasco Sauce
1 tbsp finely chopped fresh parsley
325 g/11½ oz canned sweetcorn
    kernels, drained
425 g/15 oz canned butter beans,
    drained and rinsed
2 tbsp plain flour
4 tbsp water
salt
fresh parsley sprigs, to garnish

method

1 Season the chicken pieces with salt and dust
   with paprika.

2 Heat the oil and butter in a flameproof casserole or
   large saucepan. Add the chicken pieces and cook over
   a medium heat, turning, for 10–15 minutes, or until
   golden. Transfer to a plate with a slotted spoon.

3 Add the onion and peppers to the casserole. Cook
   over a low heat, stirring occasionally, for 5 minutes,
   or until softened.

4 Add the tomatoes, wine, stock, Worcestershire sauce,
   Tabasco sauce and parsley and bring to the boil,
   stirring. Return the chicken to the casserole, cover
   and simmer, stirring occasionally, for 30 minutes.

5 Add the sweetcorn and beans to the casserole, partially
   re-cover and simmer for a further 30 minutes. Place
   the flour and water in a small bowl and mix to make
   a paste. Stir a ladleful of the cooking liquid into the
   paste, then stir the paste into the stew. Cook, stirring
   frequently, for 5 minutes. Serve, garnished with parsley.

roasted chicken with sun-blush tomato pesto

ingredients

serves 4

4 skinless, boneless chicken
   breasts, about 800 g/1 lb 12 oz
   in total
1 tbsp olive oil
salt and pepper
2 tbsp pine nuts, lightly toasted,
   to garnish

pesto

125 g/4½ oz sun-blush tomatoes
   in oil (drained weight),
   chopped
2 garlic cloves, crushed
4 tbsp pine nuts, lightly toasted
150 ml/5 fl oz extra-virgin olive oil

method

1 To make the red pesto, put the sun-blush tomatoes,
   garlic, 4 tablespoons of the pine nuts and oil into a
   food processor and process to a coarse paste.

2 Arrange the chicken in a large, ovenproof dish or
   roasting pan. Brush each breast with the oil, then place
   a tablespoon of red pesto over each breast. Using the
   back of a spoon, spread the pesto so that it covers the
   top of each breast. (Store the remaining pesto in an
   airtight container in the refrigerator for up to 1 week.)

3 Roast the chicken in a preheated oven, 200°C/400°F/
   Gas Mark 6, for 30 minutes, or until tender and the
   juices run clear when a skewer is inserted into the
   thickest part of the meat.

4 Serve sprinkled with toasted pine nuts.

variation

Add 12 stoned and finely chopped black olives (well
drained and rinsed) and ½ tablespoon of olive oil to the
pesto after processing; stir well.

roast cinnamon squab chickens with lentils

ingredients

serves 4

4 squab chickens, about
500 g/1 lb 2 oz each
2 tbsp maple syrup
1 tsp ground cinnamon
1 tbsp vegetable oil
100 ml/3½ fl oz low-salt
chicken stock
2 red onions, sliced
1 tsp cumin seeds
1 tsp coriander seeds
1 tbsp olive oil
2 garlic cloves, crushed
800 g/1 lb 12 oz canned lentils,
drained and rinsed
1 tbsp unsalted butter
2 tbsp chopped fresh parsley
pepper
steamed broccoli or green beans,
to serve (optional)

method

1 Arrange the squab chickens in a roasting pan. Mix the maple syrup, cinnamon and vegetable oil together in a small bowl and brush over the breasts of the squab chickens. Pour the stock into the roasting pan and tuck the onion slices around the birds. Roast in a preheated oven, 190°C/375°F/Gas Mark 5, for 35 minutes.

2 Meanwhile, heat a non-stick frying pan over medium heat, add the cumin and coriander seeds and cook, turning, until they start to give off an aroma. Tip into a mortar and finely crush with a pestle.

3 Heat the olive oil in a frying pan over low heat, add the garlic and spices and cook for 1–2 minutes, stirring constantly. Add the lentils to the pan and cook for 10–15 minutes, stirring occasionally.

4 Remove the chicken from the oven, and keep warm. Put the roasting pan on the hob and bring the cooking juices up to a simmer. Stir in the butter and half the parsley and season to taste with pepper.

5 To serve, divide the lentils between 4 warmed serving plates. Add a squab chicken to each plate, pour over the sauce and sprinkle with the remaining parsley. Serve with steamed broccoli or green beans, if liked.

sticky lime chicken

ingredients

serves 4

4 part-boned, skinless chicken
   breasts, about 140 g/5 oz each
grated rind and juice of 1 lime
1 tbsp honey
1 tbsp olive oil
1 garlic clove, chopped (optional)
1 tbsp chopped fresh thyme
pepper
boiled new potatoes and
   lightly cooked seasonal
   vegetables, to serve

method

1 Arrange the chicken breasts in a shallow roasting pan.

2 Put the lime rind and juice, honey, oil, garlic, if using,
   and thyme in a small bowl and combine thoroughly.
   Spoon the mixture evenly over the chicken breasts and
   season with pepper.

3 Roast the chicken in a preheated oven, 190°C/375°F/
   Gas Mark 5, basting every 10 minutes, for 35–40
   minutes, or until the chicken is tender and the juices
   run clear when a skewer is inserted into the thickest
   part of the meat. If the juices still run pink, return the
   chicken to the oven and cook for a further 5 minutes,
   then test again. As the chicken cooks, the liquid in the
   pan thickens to give a tasty, sticky coating.

4 Serve with boiled new potatoes and lightly cooked
   seasonal vegetables.

chicken with saffron mash

ingredients

serves 4

550 g/1 lb 4 oz floury potatoes,
    cut into chunks
1 garlic clove, peeled
1 tsp saffron threads, crushed
1.25 litres/2 pints chicken
    or vegetable stock
4 skinless, boneless chicken
    breasts, trimmed of all
    visible fat
2 tbsp olive oil
1 tbsp lemon juice
1 tbsp chopped fresh thyme
1 tbsp chopped fresh coriander
1 tbsp coriander seeds, crushed
100 ml/3½ fl oz hot skimmed milk
salt and pepper
fresh thyme sprigs, to garnish

method

1 Put the potatoes, garlic and saffron in a large heavy-based saucepan, add the stock and bring to the boil. Cover and simmer for 20 minutes, or until tender.

2 Meanwhile, brush the chicken breasts all over with half the olive oil and all of the lemon juice. Sprinkle with the fresh thyme and coriander and the crushed coriander seeds. Heat a griddle pan, add the chicken and cook over medium–high heat for 5 minutes on each side, or until the juices run clear when the meat is pierced with the tip of a sharp knife. Alternatively, cook the chicken breasts under a preheated medium–hot grill for 5 minutes on each side, or until cooked through.

3 Drain the potatoes and return the contents of the strainer to the pan. Add the remaining olive oil and the milk, season with salt and pepper and mash until smooth. Divide the saffron mash between 4 large, warmed serving plates, top with a piece of chicken and garnish with a few sprigs of fresh thyme. Serve.

tarragon chicken

ingredients

serves 4

4 skinless, boneless chicken
    breasts, about 175 g/6 oz each
125 ml/4 fl oz dry white wine
250–300 ml/8–10 fl oz chicken
    stock
1 garlic clove, finely chopped
1 tbsp dried tarragon
175 ml/6 fl oz double cream
1 tbsp chopped fresh tarragon
salt and pepper
fresh tarragon sprigs, to garnish

method

1 Season the chicken with salt and pepper and place in
    a single layer in a large, heavy-based frying pan. Pour
    in the wine and just enough chicken stock to cover,
    and add the garlic and dried tarragon. Bring to the
    boil, reduce the heat and cook gently for 10 minutes,
    or until the chicken is tender and cooked through.

2 Remove the chicken with a slotted spoon or tongs,
    cover and keep warm. Strain the poaching liquid into
    a clean frying pan and skim off any fat from the surface.
    Bring to the boil and cook for 12–15 minutes, or until
    reduced by about two-thirds.

3 Stir in the cream, return to the boil and cook until
    reduced by about half. Stir in the fresh tarragon. Slice
    the chicken breasts and arrange on warmed plates.
    Spoon over the sauce, garnish with tarragon sprigs
    and serve immediately.

tuscan chicken

ingredients

serves 4

2 tbsp plain flour
4 skinned chicken quarters
    or portions
3 tbsp olive oil
1 red onion, chopped
2 garlic cloves, chopped finely
1 red pepper, deseeded and
    chopped
pinch of saffron threads
150 ml/5 fl oz chicken stock or a
    mixture of chicken stock and
    dry white wine
400 g/14 oz canned tomatoes,
    chopped
4 sun-dried tomatoes in oil,
    drained and chopped
225 g/8 oz field mushrooms, sliced
115 g/4 oz black olives, pitted
4 tbsp lemon juice
salt and pepper
fresh basil leaves, to garnish
tagliatelle, fettuccine or tagliarini
    and crusty bread, to serve

method

1 Place the flour on a shallow plate and season with salt
   and pepper. Coat the chicken in the seasoned flour,
   shaking off any excess. Heat the olive oil in a large,
   flameproof casserole. Add the chicken and cook over
   medium heat, turning frequently, for 5–7 minutes,
   until golden brown. Remove from the casserole and
   set aside.

2 Add the onion, garlic and red pepper to the casserole,
   reduce the heat and cook, stirring occasionally, for
   5 minutes, until softened. Meanwhile, stir the saffron
   into the stock.

3 Stir the tomatoes, with the juice from the can, and the
   sun-dried tomatoes, mushrooms and olives into the
   casserole and cook, stirring occasionally, for 3 minutes.
   Pour in the stock and saffron mixture and the lemon
   juice. Bring to the boil, then return the chicken to
   the casserole.

4 Cover and cook in a preheated oven, 180°C/350°F/Gas
   Mark 4, for 1 hour, until the chicken is tender. Garnish
   with the basil leaves and serve immediately with pasta
   and crusty bread.

chicken with goat's cheese & basil

ingredients

serves 4

4 skinned chicken breast fillets
100 g/3½ oz soft goat's cheese
small bunch fresh basil
2 tbsp olive oil
salt and pepper

method

1 Using a sharp knife, slit along one long edge of each chicken breast, then carefully open out each breast to make a small pocket. Divide the cheese equally between the pockets and tuck three or four basil leaves in each. Close the openings and season the breasts with salt and pepper.

2 Heat the oil in a frying pan, add the chicken breasts and fry gently for 15–20 minutes, turning several times, until golden and tender.

3 Serve warm, garnished with a sprig of basil.

chicken gumbo

ingredients

serves 4–6

1 chicken, weighing 1.5 kg/3 lb
    5 oz, cut into 6 pieces
2 celery sticks, 1 broken in half
    and 1 finely chopped
1 carrot, chopped
2 onions, 1 sliced and 1 chopped
2 bay leaves
4 or groundnut oil
50 g/1¾ oz plain flour
2 large garlic cloves, crushed
1 green pepper, deseeded
    and diced
450 g/1 lb fresh okra, trimmed,
    then cut crossways into
    1-cm/½-inch slices
225 g/8 oz andouille sausage
    or Polish kielbasa, sliced
2 tbsp tomato purée
1 tsp dried thyme
½ tsp cayenne pepper
400 g/14 oz canned peeled
    plum tomatoes
salt and pepper
cooked long-grain rice, to serve

method

1 Put the chicken into a large saucepan with water to cover, and bring to the boil, skimming the surface to remove the foam. Reduce the heat to medium, add the celery stick halves, carrot, sliced onion, 1 bay leaf and ¼ teaspoon of salt and simmer for 30 minutes, or until the chicken is tender and the juices run clear when a skewer is inserted into the thickest part of the meat. Remove the chicken, straining and reserving 1 litre/1¾ pints of the liquid. Remove and discard the skin, bones and other ingredients. Cut the chicken flesh into pieces and reserve.

2 Heat the oil in a large saucepan. Over a low heat sprinkle in the flour and stir to make a roux. Add the chopped celery, chopped onion, garlic, green pepper and okra to the saucepan. Increase the heat to medium–high and cook, stirring frequently, for 5 minutes. Add the sausage and cook, stirring frequently, for 2 minutes. Stir in all the remaining ingredients, except the chicken, including the second bay leaf and the reserved cooking liquid.

3 Bring to the boil, then reduce the heat to medium–low and simmer, uncovered, for 30 minutes, stirring occasionally. Add the chicken to the saucepan and simmer for 30 minutes. Discard the bay leaf, spoon the gumbo over the rice and serve.

chicken in white wine

ingredients

serves 4

55 g/2 oz butter
2 tbsp olive oil
2 rindless, thick streaky bacon
    rashers, chopped
115 g/4 oz baby onions, peeled
1 garlic clove, finely chopped
1.8 kg/4 lb chicken pieces
400 ml/14 fl oz dry white wine
300 ml/10 fl oz chicken stock
1 bouquet garni
115 g/4 oz button mushrooms
25 g/1 oz plain flour
salt and pepper
fresh mixed herbs, to garnish

method

1 Melt half the butter with the oil in a flameproof casserole. Add the bacon and cook over a medium heat, stirring, for 5–10 minutes, or until golden brown. Transfer the bacon to a large plate. Add the onions and garlic to the casserole and cook over a low heat, stirring occasionally, for 10 minutes, or until golden. Transfer to the plate.

2 Add the chicken and cook over a medium heat, stirring constantly, for 8–10 minutes, or until golden. Transfer to the plate. Drain off any excess fat. Stir in the wine and stock and bring to the boil, scraping any sediment off the base. Add the bouquet garni and season to taste with salt and pepper. Return the bacon, onions and chicken to the casserole. Cover and cook in a preheated oven, 160°C/325°F/Gas Mark 3, for 1 hour. Add the mushrooms, re-cover and cook for 15 minutes. Meanwhile, make a beurre manié by mashing the remaining butter with the flour in a small bowl.

3 Remove the casserole from the oven and set over a medium heat. Remove and discard the bouquet garni. Whisk in the beurre manié, a little at a time. Bring to the boil, stirring, then serve, garnished with fresh herb sprigs.

chicken tagine

ingredients

serves 4

1 tbsp olive oil
1 onion, cut into small wedges
2–4 garlic cloves, sliced
450 g/1 lb skinless, boneless
  chicken breast, diced
1 tsp ground cumin
2 cinnamon sticks, lightly bruised
1 tbsp plain wholemeal flour
225 g/8 oz aubergine, diced
1 red pepper, deseeded and
  chopped
85 g/3 oz button mushrooms,
  sliced
1 tbsp tomato purée
600 ml/1 pint chicken stock
280 g/10 oz canned chickpeas,
  drained and rinsed
55 g/2 oz ready-to-eat dried
  apricots, chopped
salt and pepper
1 tbsp chopped fresh coriander,
  to garnish

method

1 Heat the oil in a large saucepan over a medium heat, add the onion and garlic and cook for 3 minutes, stirring frequently. Add the chicken and cook, stirring constantly, for a further 5 minutes, or until sealed on all sides. Add the cumin and cinnamon sticks to the saucepan halfway through sealing the chicken.

2 Sprinkle in the flour and cook, stirring constantly, for 2 minutes.

3 Add the aubergine, red pepper and mushrooms and cook for a further 2 minutes, stirring constantly. Blend the tomato purée with the stock, stir into the saucepan and bring to the boil. Reduce the heat and add the chickpeas and apricots. Cover and simmer for 15–20 minutes, or until the chicken is tender.

4 Season with salt and pepper to taste and serve immediately, sprinkled with coriander.

florida chicken

ingredients

serves 4

450 g/1 lb skinless, boneless chicken

1½ tbsp plain flour

1 tbsp olive oil

1 onion, cut into wedges

2 celery sticks, sliced

150 ml/5 fl oz orange juice

300 ml/10 fl oz chicken stock

1 tbsp light soy sauce

1–2 tsp clear honey

1 tbsp grated orange rind

1 orange pepper, deseeded and chopped

225 g/8 oz courgettes, sliced into half moons

2 small corn cobs, halved

1 orange, peeled and segmented

salt and pepper

1 tbsp chopped fresh parsley, to garnish

method

1 Lightly rinse the chicken and pat dry with kitchen paper. Cut into bite-sized pieces. Season the flour well with salt and pepper. Toss the chicken in the seasoned flour until well coated and reserve any remaining seasoned flour.

2 Heat the oil in a large heavy-based frying pan and cook the chicken over a high heat, stirring frequently, for 5 minutes, or until golden on all sides and sealed. Using a slotted spoon, transfer the chicken to a plate. Add the onion and celery to the frying pan and cook over a medium heat, stirring frequently, for 5 minutes, or until softened. Sprinkle in the reserved seasoned flour and cook, stirring constantly, for 2 minutes, then remove from the heat. Gradually stir in the orange juice, stock, soy sauce and honey, followed by the orange rind, then return to the heat and bring to the boil, stirring.

3 Return the chicken to the frying pan. Reduce the heat, cover and simmer, stirring occasionally, for 15 minutes. Add the orange pepper, courgettes and corn cobs and simmer for a further 10 minutes, or until the chicken and vegetables are tender. Add the orange segments, stir well and heat for 1 minute. Serve, garnished with the parsley.

mexican chicken, chilli & potato pot

ingredients

serves 4

2 tbsp vegetable oil
450 g/1 lb skinless, boneless
    chicken breasts, cubed
1 onion, finely chopped
1 green pepper, deseeded and
    finely chopped
1 potato, diced
1 sweet potato, diced
2 garlic cloves, very finely chopped
1–2 fresh green chillies, deseeded
    and very finely chopped
200 g/7 oz canned chopped
    tomatoes
½ tsp dried oregano
½ tsp salt
¼ tsp pepper
4 tbsp chopped fresh coriander
450 ml/16 fl oz chicken stock

method

1 Heat the oil in a large heavy-based saucepan over a
   medium–high heat. Add the chicken and cook until
   lightly browned. Reduce the heat to medium. Add the
   onion, pepper, potato and sweet potato. Cover and
   cook, stirring occasionally, for 5 minutes, or until the
   vegetables begin to soften.

2 Add the garlic and chillies and cook for 1 minute.
   Stir in the tomatoes, oregano, salt, pepper and half
   the coriander and cook for 1 minute. Pour in the
   stock. Bring to the boil, then cover and simmer over
   a medium–low heat for 15–20 minutes, or until the
   chicken is cooked through and the vegetables
   are tender.

3 Sprinkle with the remaining coriander just before
   serving.

coq au vin

ingredients

serves 4

2 tbsp butter
8 baby onions
125 g/4½ oz bacon, roughly
    chopped
4 chicken joints
1 garlic clove, finely chopped
12 white mushrooms
300 ml/10 fl oz red wine
bouquet garni sachet
1 tbsp chopped fresh tarragon
salt and pepper
2 tsp cornflour
1–2 tbsp cold water
fresh flat-leaf parsley sprigs,
    to garnish
sautéed sliced potatoes, to serve

method

1 Melt half of the butter in a large frying pan over medium heat. Add the onions and bacon and cook, stirring, for 3 minutes. Lift out the bacon and onions and reserve.

2 Melt the remaining butter in the pan and add the chicken joints. Cook for 3 minutes, then turn over and cook on the other side for 2 minutes. Drain off some of the chicken fat, then return the bacon and onions to the pan. Add the garlic, mushrooms, red wine, bouquet garni and tarragon. Season with salt and pepper. Cook for about 1 hour, or until the chicken is cooked through.

3 Remove the pan from the heat, lift out the chicken, onions, bacon and mushrooms, transfer them to a serving platter and keep the dish warm. Discard the bouquet garni.

4 Mix the cornflour with enough of the water to make a paste, then stir into the juices in the pan. Bring to the boil, reduce the heat and cook, stirring, for 1 minute. Pour the sauce over the chicken, garnish with parsley sprigs and serve with sautéed sliced potatoes.

spanish chicken with preserved lemons

ingredients

serves 4

1 tbsp plain flour
4 chicken quarters, skin on
2 tbsp olive oil
2 garlic cloves, crushed
1 large Spanish onion, thinly sliced
750 ml/1¼ pints low-salt chicken
    stock
½ tsp saffron threads
2 yellow peppers, deseeded
    and cut into chunks
2 preserved lemons, cut into
    quarters
250 g/9 oz brown basmati rice
white pepper
12 pimiento-stuffed green olives
chopped fresh parsley, to garnish
salad leaves, to serve (optional)

method

1 Put the flour into a large freezer bag. Add the chicken, close the top of the bag and shake to coat with flour.

2 Heat the oil in a large frying pan over low heat, add the garlic and cook for 1 minute, stirring constantly. Add the chicken to the pan and cook over medium heat, turning frequently, for 5 minutes, or until the skin has lightly browned, then remove to a plate. Add the onion to the pan and cook, stirring occasionally, for 10 minutes until soft.

3 Meanwhile, put the stock and saffron into a saucepan over low heat and heat through.

4 Transfer the chicken and onion to a large casserole dish, add the yellow peppers, lemons and rice, then pour over the stock. Mix well and season with pepper.

5 Cover and cook in a preheated oven, 180°C/350°F/Gas Mark 4, for 50 minutes, or until the chicken is cooked through and tender. Reduce the oven temperature to 160°C/325°F/Gas Mark 3. Add the olives to the casserole and cook for a further 10 minutes.

6 Serve the dish sprinkled with chopped parsley and accompanied by salad greens, if using.

louisiana chicken

ingredients

serves 4

5 tbsp corn oil
4 chicken portions
6 tbsp plain flour
1 onion, chopped
2 celery stalks, sliced
1 green pepper, deseeded
    and chopped
2 garlic cloves, finely chopped
2 tsp chopped fresh thyme
2 fresh red chillies, deseeded
    and finely chopped
400 g/14 oz canned
    chopped tomatoes
300 ml/10 fl oz chicken stock
salt and pepper
lamb's lettuce and chopped
    fresh thyme, to garnish

method

1 Heat the oil in a large, heavy-based saucepan or
   flameproof casserole. Add the chicken and cook over
   medium heat, stirring, for 5–10 minutes, or until golden.
   Transfer the chicken to a plate with a perforated spoon.

2 Stir the flour into the oil and cook over very low heat,
   stirring constantly, for 15 minutes, or until light golden.
   Do not let it burn. Add the onion, celery and green
   pepper and cook, stirring constantly, for 2 minutes.
   Add the garlic, thyme and chillies and cook, stirring,
   for 1 minute.

3 Stir in the tomatoes and their juices, then gradually
   stir in the stock. Return the chicken pieces to the pan,
   cover and simmer for 45 minutes, or until the chicken
   is cooked through and tender. Season with salt and
   pepper, transfer to warmed serving plates and serve
   immediately, garnished with lamb's lettuce and a
   sprinkling of chopped thyme.

red hot chilli chicken

ingredients

serves 4

1 tbsp curry paste
2 fresh green chillies, chopped
5 dried red chillies
2 tbsp tomato purée
2 garlic cloves, chopped
1 tsp chilli powder
pinch of sugar
pinch of salt
2 tbsp peanut or corn oil
½ tsp cumin seeds
1 onion, chopped
2 curry leaves
1 tsp ground cumin
1 tsp ground coriander
½ tsp ground turmeric
400 g/14 oz canned chopped
    tomatoes
150 ml/5 fl oz chicken stock
4 skinless, boneless chicken breasts
1 tsp garam masala
freshly cooked rice and plain
    yogurt garnished with
    mint sprigs and diced
    cucumber, to serve

method

1 To make the chilli paste, place the curry paste, fresh and dried chillies, tomato purée, garlic, chilli powder and sugar in a blender or food processor with the salt. Process to a smooth paste.

2 Heat the oil in a large, heavy-based saucepan. Add the cumin seeds and cook over medium heat, stirring constantly, for 2 minutes, or until they begin to pop and release their aroma. Add the onion and curry leaves and cook, stirring, for 5 minutes.

3 Add the chilli paste, cook for 2 minutes, then stir in the ground cumin, coriander and turmeric and cook for a further 2 minutes.

4 Add the tomatoes and their juices and the stock. Bring to the boil, then reduce the heat and simmer for 5 minutes. Add the chicken and garam masala, cover, and simmer gently for 20 minutes, or until the chicken is cooked through and tender. Serve immediately with freshly cooked rice and yogurt garnished with mint sprigs and diced cucumber.

chicken cacciatore

ingredients

serves 4

3 tbsp olive oil
1.8 kg/4 lb skinless chicken pieces
2 red onions, sliced
2 garlic cloves, finely chopped
400 g/14 oz canned chopped
    tomatoes
2 tbsp chopped fresh flat-leaf
    parsley
1 tbsp sun-dried tomato purée
150 ml/5 fl oz red wine
6 fresh basil leaves
salt and pepper
fresh basil sprigs, to garnish
pasta, to serve

method

1 Heat the olive oil in a flameproof casserole. Add the chicken and cook over a medium heat, stirring frequently, for 5–10 minutes, or until golden. Transfer to a plate with a slotted spoon.

2 Add the onions and garlic to the casserole and cook over a low heat, stirring occasionally, for 10 minutes, or until golden. Add the tomatoes, the parsley, tomato purée and wine, and tear in the basil leaves. Season to taste with salt and pepper.

3 Bring the mixture to the boil, then return the chicken to the casserole, pushing it down into the cooking liquid. Cover and cook in a preheated oven, 160°C/325°F/Gas Mark 3 for 1 hour, or until the chicken is cooked through and tender. Garnish with fresh basil sprigs and serve immediately with pasta.

steamed chicken with chilli & coriander butter

ingredients

serves 4

50 g/2 oz butter, softened
1 fresh Thai chilli, seeded and
     chopped
3 tbsp chopped fresh coriander
4 skinless, boneless
     chicken breasts, about
     175 g/6 oz each
400 ml/14 fl oz coconut milk
350 ml/12 fl oz chicken stock
200 g/7 oz basmati rice

pickled vegetables

1 carrot
½ cucumber
3 spring onions
2 tbsp rice vinegar
salt and pepper

method

1 Mix the butter with the chile and coriander. Cut a deep slash into the side of each chicken breast to form a pocket. Spoon quarter of the flavoured butter into each pocket and place on a 30-cm/12-inch square of baking parchment.

2 Season to taste with salt and pepper, then bring together 2 opposite sides of the paper on top, folding over to seal firmly. Twist the ends to seal. Pour the coconut milk and stock into a large pan with a steamer top. Bring to a boil.

3 Stir in the rice with a pinch of salt. Put the chicken parcels in the steamer top, cover, and simmer for 15–18 minutes, stirring the rice once, until the rice is tender and the chicken is cooked through. Meanwhile, peel the carrot, then trim the carrot, cucumber and spring onions and cut into fine sticks. Sprinkle with the vinegar.

4 Unwrap the chicken, reserving the juices, and cut in half diagonally. Serve the chicken on the rice, with the juices spooned over and pickled vegetables on the side.

baked tapenade chicken

ingredients

serves 4

4 skinless, boneless chicken breasts
4 tbsp green olive tapenade
8 thin slices smoked pancetta
2 garlic cloves, coarsely chopped
250 g/ 9 oz cherry tomatoes,
   halved
125 ml/4 fl oz cup dry white wine
2 tbsp olive oil
8 slices ciabatta
salt and pepper

method

1 Put the chicken breasts on a cutting board and cut three deep slashes into each. Spread a tablespoon of the tapenade over each chicken breast, pushing it into the slashes with a palette knife.

2 Wrap each chicken breast in two slices of pancetta. Place the chicken breasts in a shallow ovenproof dish and arrange the garlic and tomatoes around them. Season to taste with salt and pepper, then pour over the wine and 1 tablespoon of the oil.

3 Bake in a preheated oven, 220°C/425°F/Gas Mark 7, for about 20 minutes, until the juices run clear when the chicken is pierced with a skewer. Cover the dish loosely with aluminum foil and let stand for 5 minutes.

4 Brush the ciabatta with the remaining oil and cook on under a hot preheated grill, for 2–3 minutes, turning once, until golden.

5 Transfer the chicken and tomatoes to serving plates and spoon over the juices. Serve the dish with the toasted ciabatta.

pistachio chicken korma

ingredients

serves 4

115 g/4 oz shelled pistachio nuts,
   soaked in boiling water for
   20 minutes
200 ml/7 fl oz boiling water
good pinch of saffron threads,
   pounded and soaked in 2 tbsp
   hot milk
700 g/1 lb 9 oz skinless, boneless
   chicken breasts or thighs, cut
   into 2.5-cm/1-inch cubes
1 tsp salt, or to taste
½ tsp pepper
juice of ½ lemon
55 g/2 oz ghee or unsalted butter
6 green cardamom pods
1 large onion, finely chopped
2 tsp garlic purée
2 tsp ginger purée
1 tbsp ground coriander
½ tsp chilli powder
280 g/10 oz whole milk natural
   yogurt, whisked
150 ml/5 fl oz single cream
2 tbsp rosewater
6–8 white rose petals, to garnish
freshly cooked basmati rice and
   lemon wedges, to serve

method

1 Put the chicken in a non-metallic bowl and add the salt, pepper and lemon juice. Rub into the chicken, cover, keep cool, and leave to marinate for 30 minutes.

2 Melt the ghee in a medium heavy-based saucepan over a low heat and add the cardamom pods. When they have puffed up, add the onion and increase the heat to medium. Cook, stirring frequently, until the onion is a pale golden colour. Add the garlic and ginger purées and cook, stirring frequently, for a further 2–3 minutes. Add the coriander and chilli powder and cook, stirring, for 30 seconds. Add the chicken, increase the heat to medium–high and cook, stirring constantly, for 5–6 minutes, until it changes colour.

3 Reduce the heat to low and add the yogurt and the saffron and milk mixture. Bring to a slow simmer, cover and cook for 15 minutes. Stir halfway through to ensure that it does not stick to the base of the pan.

4 Meanwhile, put the pistachio nuts and their soaking water in a blender or food processor and process until smooth. Add to the chicken mixture, followed by the cream. Cover and simmer, stirring occasionally, for a further 15–20 minutes. Stir in the rosewater and remove from the heat. Garnish with the rose petals and serve with basmati rice and lemon wedges.

chicken with walnut sauce

ingredients

serves 4

4–8 skinned chicken pieces
1/2 lemon, cut into wedges
3 tbsp olive oil
150 ml/5 fl oz dry white wine
300 ml/10 fl oz chicken stock
1 bay leaf
100 g/1/2 oz walnut pieces
2 garlic cloves
150 ml/5 fl oz Greek-style yogurt
salt and pepper
chopped fresh flat-leaf parsley,
    to garnish
rice or pilaf and pitta bread,
    to serve

method

1 Rub the chicken pieces with the lemon. Heat the oil in a large frying pan, add the chicken pieces and fry quickly until lightly browned on all sides.

2 Pour the wine into the pan and bring to the boil. Add the stock, bay leaf, salt and pepper and simmer for about 20 minutes, turning several times, until the chicken is tender.

3 Meanwhile, put the walnuts and garlic in a food processor and blend to form a fairly smooth purée.

4 When the chicken is cooked, transfer to a warmed serving dish and keep warm. Stir the walnut mixture and yogurt into the pan juices and heat gently for about 5 minutes until the sauce is quite thick. (Do not boil or the sauce will curdle.) Season with salt and pepper.

5 Pour the walnut sauce over the chicken pieces and serve hot with rice or pilaf and pitta bread. Garnish with chopped fresh parsley.

chicken kiev

ingredients

serves 4

4 tbsp butter, softened
1 garlic clove, finely chopped
1 tbsp finely chopped fresh parsley
1 tbsp finely chopped fresh
    oregano
4 skinless, boneless chicken breasts
85 g/3 oz fresh white or
    wholewheat breadcrumbs
3 tbsp freshly grated Parmesan
    cheese
1 egg, beaten
250 ml/9 fl oz vegetable oil,
    for deep-frying
salt and pepper
slices of lemon and flat-leaf parsley
    sprigs, to garnish
freshly cooked new potatoes and
    selection of cooked vegetables,
    to serve

method

1 Place the butter and garlic in a bowl and mix together well. Stir in the chopped herbs and season well with salt and pepper. Pound the chicken breasts to flatten them to an even thickness, then place a tablespoon of herb butter in the centre of each one. Fold in the sides to enclose the butter, then secure with wooden cocktail sticks.

2 Combine the breadcrumbs and grated Parmesan on a plate. Dip the chicken parcels into the beaten egg, then coat in the breadcrumb mixture. Transfer to a plate, cover and chill for 30 minutes. Remove from the refrigerator and coat in the egg and then the breadcrumb mixture for a second time.

3 Pour the oil into a deep-fryer to a depth that will cover the chicken parcels. Heat until it reaches 180–190°C/350–375°F, or until a cube of bread browns in 30 seconds. Transfer the chicken to the hot oil and deep-fry for 5 minutes, or until cooked through. Lift out the chicken and drain on kitchen paper.

4 Divide the chicken between 4 serving plates, garnish with lemon slices and parsley sprigs and serve with new potatoes and a selection of vegetables.

chicken fricassée

ingredients

serves 4

1 tbsp plain flour
salt and white pepper
4 skinless, boneless chicken
    breasts, about 140 g/5 oz each,
    trimmed of all visible fat and
    cut into 2-cm/¾-inch cubes
1 tbsp sunflower or corn oil
8 pearl onions
2 garlic cloves, crushed
250 ml/8 fl oz chicken stock
2 carrots, diced
2 celery stalks, diced
225 g/8 oz frozen peas
1 yellow pepper, deseeded
    and diced
115 g/4 oz white mushrooms,
    sliced
125 ml/4 fl oz low-fat plain yogurt
3 tbsp chopped fresh parsley

method

1 Spread out the flour on a dish and season with salt and
  pepper. Add the chicken and, using your hands, coat in
  the flour. Heat the oil in a heavy-based saucepan. Add
  the onions and garlic and cook over low heat, stirring
  occasionally, for 5 minutes. Add the chicken and cook,
  stirring, for 10 minutes, or until just beginning to colour.

2 Gradually stir in the stock, then add the carrots, celery
  and peas. Bring to the boil, then reduce the heat,
  cover and simmer for 5 minutes. Add the pepper and
  mushrooms, cover and simmer for a further 10 minutes.

3 Stir in the yogurt and chopped parsley and season
  with salt and pepper. Cook for 1–2 minutes, or until
  heated through, then transfer to 4 large, warmed
  serving plates and serve immediately.

noodles
& pasta

noodle basket with chicken-lime salad

ingredients

serves 4

peanut or corn oil, for deep-frying
and oiling
250 g/9 oz fresh thin or medium
Chinese egg noodles

chicken-lime salad

6 tbsp sour cream
6 tbsp mayonnaise
2.5-cm/1-inch piece fresh ginger,
peeled and grated
grated rind and juice of 1 lime
4 skinless, boneless chicken thighs,
poached and cooled, then cut
into thin strips
1 carrot, peeled and grated
1 cucumber, cut in half
lengthways, deseeded
and sliced
1 tbsp finely chopped fresh
coriander
1 tbsp finely chopped
fresh mint
1 tbsp finely chopped fresh parsley
several fresh basil leaves, torn
salt and pepper

method

1 To shape noodle baskets, you will need a special set of 2 long-handled wire baskets that clip inside each other, available from gourmet kitchen stores. Dip the larger wire basket in oil, then line it completely and evenly with one-quarter of the tangled noodles. Dip the smaller wire basket in oil, then position it inside the larger basket and clip it into position.

2 Heat 10 cm/4 inches of oil in a wok or deep-fat fryer to 180–190°C/350–375°F, or until a cube of bread browns in 30 seconds. Lower the baskets into the oil and deep-fry for 2–3 minutes, or until the noodles are golden brown. Remove the baskets from the oil and drain on kitchen paper. Unclip the 2 wire baskets and carefully remove the small one. Use a round-bladed knife, if necessary, to prise the noodle basket from the wire frame. Repeat to make 3 more baskets. Let the noodle baskets cool.

3 To make the salad, combine the sour cream, mayonnaise, ginger and lime rind. Gradually add the lime juice until you get the flavour you like. Stir in the chicken, carrot, cucumber, salt and pepper. Cover and let chill. Just before serving, stir in the herbs and spoon the salad into the noodle

yaki soba

ingredients

serves 2

400 g/14 oz ramen noodles
1 onion, finely sliced
200 g/7 oz fresh beansprouts
1 red pepper, deseeded and
    thinly sliced
1 boneless, skin-on cooked chicken
    breast, about 150 g/5½ oz,
    sliced
12 cooked peeled prawns
1 tbsp groundnut oil
2 tbsp shoyu (Japanese soy sauce)
½ tbsp mirin
1 tsp sesame oil
1 tsp toasted sesame seeds
2 spring onions, finely sliced

method

1 Cook the noodles according to the instructions on the
   packet. Drain well, and tip into a bowl.

2 Mix the onion, beansprouts, red pepper, chicken and
   prawns together in a separate bowl. Stir through
   the noodles.

3 Heat a wok over a high heat, then add the groundnut
   oil. Add the noodle mixture and stir-fry for 4 minutes,
   or until golden, then add the shoyu, mirin and sesame
   oil and toss together.

4 Divide the mixture between 2 bowls, sprinkle with
   the sesame seeds and spring onions and serve
   immediately.

teriyaki chicken with sesame noodles

ingredients

serves 4

4 boneless chicken breasts, about
175 g/6 oz each, with or
without skin, as you wish
about 4 tbsp bottled teriyaki sauce
peanut or corn oil
cucumber fans, to garnish

sesame noodles
250 g/9 oz dried thin buckwheat
noodles
1 tbsp toasted sesame oil
2 tbsp toasted sesame seeds
2 tbsp finely chopped fresh parsley
salt and pepper

method

1 Using a sharp knife, score each chicken breast
diagonally across 3 times and rub all over with teriyaki
sauce. Set aside to marinate for at least 10 minutes.

2 When you are ready to cook the chicken, preheat the
grill to high. Bring a saucepan of water to the boil, add
the buckwheat noodles and boil for 3 minutes, or
according to the packet instructions, until soft. Drain
and rinse well in cold water to stop the cooking and
remove excess starch, then drain again.

3 Lightly brush the grill rack with oil. Add the chicken
breasts, skin-side up, and brush again with a little extra
teriyaki sauce. Grill the chicken breasts about 10 cm/
4 inches from the heat, brushing occasionally with
extra teriyaki sauce, for 15 minutes, or until cooked
through and the juices run clear.

4 Meanwhile, heat a wok or large frying pan over high
heat. Add the sesame oil and heat until it shimmers.
Add the noodles and stir around to heat through, then
stir in the sesame seeds and parsley. Season with salt
and pepper. To serve, transfer the chicken breasts to
plates and add a portion of noodles to each. Garnish
with cucumber fans.

chicken chow mein

ingredients

serves 4

250 g/9 oz packet medium
  egg noodles
2 tbsp sunflower oil
280 g/10 oz cooked chicken
  breasts, shredded
1 garlic clove, finely chopped
1 red pepper, deseeded
  and thinly sliced
100 g/3½ oz shiitake
  mushrooms, sliced
6 spring onions, sliced
100 g/3½ oz beansprouts
3 tbsp soy sauce
1 tbsp sesame oil

method

1 Place the egg noodles in a large bowl or dish and
  break them up slightly. Pour enough boiling water over
  the noodles to cover and let stand while preparing the
  other ingredients.

2 Preheat a wok over medium heat. Add the sunflower
  oil and swirl it around to coat the sides of the wok.
  When the oil is hot, add the shredded chicken, garlic,
  pepper, mushrooms, spring onions and beansprouts
  to the wok and stir-fry for about 5 minutes.

3 Drain the noodles thoroughly then add them to the
  wok, toss well, and stir-fry for a further 5 minutes.
  Drizzle the soy sauce and sesame oil over the chow
  mein and toss until well combined.

4 Transfer the chicken chow mein to warmed serving
  bowls and serve immediately.

variation

Add 1 teaspoon of Chinese five spice to the wok just
before you add the chicken, and stir for a few seconds
to release the aromas.

chicken & green vegetables

ingredients

serves 4

250 g/9 oz dried medium Chinese
    egg noodles
2 tbsp peanut or corn oil
1 large garlic clove, crushed
1 fresh green chilli, deseeded
    and sliced
1 tbsp Chinese five-spice powder
2 skinless, boneless chicken
    breasts, cut into thin strips
2 green peppers, cored, deseeded
    and sliced
115 g/4 oz broccoli, cut into
    small florets
55 g/2 oz green beans, trimmed
    and cut into 4-cm/1½-inch
    pieces
5 tbsp vegetable or chicken stock
2 tbsp bottled oyster sauce
2 tbsp soy sauce
1 tbsp Shaoxing rice wine
    or dry sherry
55 g/2 oz beansprouts

method

1 Cook the noodles in a saucepan of boiling water for
   4 minutes, or according to the packet instructions,
   until soft. Drain, rinse and drain again, then set aside.

2 Heat a wok or large frying pan over high heat. Add
   1 tablespoon of the oil and heat until it shimmers.
   Add the garlic, chilli and five-spice powder and stir-fry
   for about 30 seconds.

3 Add the chicken and stir-fry for 3 minutes, or until it is
   cooked through. Use a slotted spoon to remove the
   chicken from the wok and set aside.

4 Add the remaining oil to the wok and heat until it
   shimmers. Add the peppers, broccoli and beans and
   stir-fry for about 2 minutes. Stir in the stock, oyster
   sauce, soy sauce and rice wine and return the chicken
   to the wok. Continue stir-frying for about 1 minute,
   until the chicken is reheated and the vegetables are
   tender, but still firm to the bite. Add the noodles
   and beansprouts and use 2 forks to mix all the
   ingredients together.

pappardelle with chicken & ceps

ingredients

serves 4

40 g/1½ oz dried cep mushrooms
175 ml/6 fl oz hot water
800 g/1 lb 12 oz canned chopped
    tomatoes
1 fresh red chilli, deseeded and
    finely chopped
3 tbsp olive oil
350 g/12 oz skinless, boneless
    chicken, cut into thin strips
2 garlic cloves, finely chopped
350 g/12 oz dried pappardelle
salt and pepper
2 tbsp chopped fresh flat-leaf
    parsley, to garnish

method

1 Place the ceps in a small bowl, add the hot water and soak for 30 minutes. Meanwhile, place the tomatoes and their juices in a heavy-based saucepan and break them up, then stir in the chilli. Bring to the boil, then reduce the heat and simmer, stirring occasionally, for 30 minutes, or until reduced.

2 Remove the mushrooms from their soaking liquid with a slotted spoon, reserving the liquid. Strain the liquid into the tomatoes through a coffee filter paper, or a sieve lined with cheesecloth, and simmer for 15 minutes.

3 Meanwhile, heat 2 tablespoons of the olive oil in a heavy-based frying pan. Add the chicken and cook, stirring frequently, until golden brown all over and tender. Stir in the mushrooms and garlic and cook for a further 5 minutes.

4 While the chicken is cooking, bring a large, heavy-based saucepan of lightly salted water to the boil. Add the pasta, return to the boil and cook for 8–10 minutes, or until tender but still firm to the bite. Drain well, then transfer to a warmed serving dish. Drizzle with the remaining olive oil and toss lightly. Stir the chicken mixture into the tomato sauce, season and spoon onto the pasta. Toss lightly, sprinkle with parsley and serve at once.

spaghetti with parsley chicken

ingredients

serves 4

1 tbsp olive oil
thinly pared rind of 1 lemon,
    cut into julienne strips
1 tsp finely chopped fresh ginger
1 tsp sugar
salt
250 ml/8 fl oz chicken stock
250 g/9 oz dried spaghetti
4 tbsp butter
225 g/8 oz skinless, boneless
    chicken breasts, diced
1 red onion, finely chopped
leaves from 2 bunches of
    flat-leaf parsley

method

1 Heat the olive oil in a heavy-based saucepan. Add the lemon rind and cook over low heat, stirring frequently, for 5 minutes. Stir in the ginger and sugar, season with salt and cook, stirring constantly, for a further 2 minutes. Pour in the chicken stock, bring to the boil, then cook for 5 minutes, or until the liquid has reduced by half.

2 Meanwhile, bring a large heavy-based saucepan of lightly salted water to the boil. Add the pasta, return to the boil and cook for 8–10 minutes, or until tender but still firm to the bite.

3 Meanwhile, melt half the butter in a frying pan. Add the chicken and onion and cook, stirring frequently, for 5 minutes, or until the chicken is light brown all over. Stir in the lemon and ginger mixture and cook for 1 minute. Stir in the parsley leaves and cook, stirring constantly, for a further 3 minutes.

4 Drain the pasta and transfer to a warmed serving dish, then add the remaining butter and toss well. Add the chicken sauce, toss again and serve.

pasta with chicken & feta

ingredients

serves 4

2 tbsp olive oil
450 g/1 lb skinless, boneless
    chicken breasts, cut into
    thin strips
6 spring onions, chopped
225 g/8 oz Feta cheese, diced
4 tbsp chopped fresh chives
450 g/1 lb dried garganelli
salt and pepper
tomato focaccia, to serve

method

1 Heat the olive oil in a heavy-based frying pan.
   Add the chicken and cook over medium heat, stirring
   frequently, for 5–8 minutes, or until golden all over and
   cooked through. Add the spring onions and cook for
   2 minutes. Stir the Feta cheese into the pan with half
   the chives and season with salt and pepper.

2 Meanwhile, bring a large heavy-based saucepan of
   lightly salted water to the boil. Add the pasta, return to
   the boil and cook for 8–10 minutes, or until tender but
   still firm to the bite. Drain well, then transfer to a
   warmed serving dish.

3 Spoon the chicken mixture onto the pasta, toss lightly
   and serve immediately, garnished with the remaining
   chives and accompanied by tomato focaccia.

chicken with creamy penne

ingredients

serves 2

200 g/7 oz dried penne
1 tbsp olive oil
2 skinless, boneless chicken breasts
4 tbsp dry white wine
115 g/4 oz frozen peas
5 tbsp double cream
salt
4–5 tbsp chopped fresh parsley,
    to garnish

method

1 Bring a large saucepan of lightly salted water to the boil. Add the pasta, bring back to the boil and cook for about 8–10 minutes, until tender but still firm to the bite.

2 Meanwhile, heat the oil in a frying pan, add the chicken and cook over a medium heat for about 4 minutes on each side.

3 Pour in the wine and cook over a high heat until it has almost evaporated. Drain the pasta. Add the peas, cream and pasta to the frying pan and stir well. Cover and simmer for 2 minutes. Garnish with fresh parsley and serve.

chicken with linguine & artichokes

ingredients

serves 4

4 chicken breasts, skinned
finely grated rind and juice
　of 1 lemon
2 tbsp olive oil
2 garlic cloves, crushed
400 g/14 oz canned artichoke
　hearts, drained and sliced
250 g/9 oz baby plum tomatoes
300 g/10½ oz dried linguine
chopped fresh parsley and finely
　grated Parmesan cheese,
　to garnish

method

1 Put each chicken breast in turn between 2 pieces of clingfilm and bash with a rolling pin to flatten. Put the chicken into a shallow, non-metallic dish with the lemon rind and juice and 1 tablespoon of the oil and turn to coat in the marinade. Cover and marinate in the refrigerator for 30 minutes.

2 Heat the remaining oil in a frying pan over low heat, add the garlic and cook for 1 minute, stirring frequently. Add the artichokes and tomatoes and cook for 5 minutes, stirring occasionally. Add about half the marinade from the chicken and cook over medium heat for a further 5 minutes.

3 Preheat the grill to high. Remove the chicken from the remaining marinade and arrange on the grill pan. Cook the chicken under the preheated grill for 5 minutes each side until thoroughly cooked through. Meanwhile, add the linguine to a saucepan of boiling water and cook for 7–9 minutes, or until just tender.

4 Drain the pasta and return to the pan, pour over the artichoke and tomato mixture and slice in the cooked chicken. Divide between 4 warmed plates and sprinkle over the parsley and cheese.

chicken lasagna

ingredients

serves 6

2 tbsp olive oil
900 g/2 lb fresh ground chicken
1 garlic clove, finely chopped
4 carrots, chopped
4 leeks, sliced
500 ml/16 fl oz chicken stock
2 tbsp tomato purée
115 g/4 oz Cheddar cheese, grated
1 tsp Dijon mustard
625 ml/1 pint hot béchamel sauce
115 g/4 oz dried no-precook
    lasagna
salt and pepper

béchamel sauce

625 ml/1 pint milk
1 bay leaf
6 black peppercorns
2 slices of onion
mace blade
4 tbsp butter
6 tbsp plain flour
salt and pepper
wild rocket and Parmesan
    shavings, to serve

method

1 To make the béchamel sauce, pour the milk into a saucepan and add the bay leaf, peppercorns, onion and mace. Heat gently to just below boiling point, then remove from the heat, cover, infuse for 10 minutes, then strain. Melt the butter in a separate saucepan. Sprinkle in the flour and cook over low heat, stirring constantly, for 1 minute. Gradually stir in the milk, then bring to the boil and cook, stirring, until thickened and smooth. Season.

2 Heat the oil in a heavy-based saucepan. Add the chicken and cook over medium heat, breaking it up with a wooden spoon, for 5 minutes, or until browned all over. Add the garlic, carrots and leeks, and cook, stirring occasionally, for 5 minutes. Stir in the chicken stock and tomato purée and season with salt and pepper. Bring to the boil, reduce the heat, cover and simmer for 30 minutes.

3 Whisk half the Cheddar cheese and the mustard into the hot béchamel sauce. In a large ovenproof dish, make alternate layers of the chicken mixture, lasagna and cheese sauce, ending with a layer of cheese sauce. Sprinkle with the remaining Cheddar cheese and bake in a preheated oven, 190°C/375°F/Gas Mark 5, for 1 hour, or until golden brown and bubbling. Serve immediately, with rocket and Parmesan shavings.

chicken & wild mushroom cannelloni

ingredients

serves 4

2 tbsp olive oil

2 garlic cloves, crushed

1 large onion, finely chopped

225 g/8 oz wild mushrooms, sliced

350 g/12 oz ground chicken

115 g/4 oz prosciutto, diced

150 ml/5 fl oz Marsala wine

200 g/7 oz canned chopped
    tomatoes

1 tbsp shredded
    fresh basil leaves

2 tbsp tomato purée

10–12 dried cannelloni tubes

butter, for greasing

625 ml/1 pint béchamel sauce (see
    page 170)

85 g/3 oz freshly grated Parmesan
    cheese

salt and pepper

method

1 Heat the olive oil in a heavy-based frying pan. Add the garlic, onion and mushrooms and cook over low heat, stirring frequently, for 8–10 minutes. Add the ground chicken and prosciutto and cook, stirring frequently, for 12 minutes, or until browned all over. Stir in the Marsala, tomatoes and their can juices, basil and tomato purée and cook for 4 minutes. Season with salt and pepper, then cover and simmer for 30 minutes. Uncover, stir and simmer for 15 minutes.

2 Meanwhile, bring a large, heavy-based saucepan of lightly salted water to the boil. Add the pasta, return to the boil and cook for 8–10 minutes, or until tender but still firm to the bite. Using a slotted spoon, transfer the pasta to a plate and pat dry with paper towels.

3 Using a teaspoon, fill the cannelloni tubes with the chicken, prosciutto and mushroom mixture. Transfer them to a large, lightly greased ovenproof dish. Pour the béchamel sauce over them to cover completely and sprinkle with the grated Parmesan cheese.

4 Bake the cannelloni in a preheated oven, 190°C/375°F/ Gas Mark 5, for 30 minutes, or until golden brown and bubbling. Serve at once.

rice

chicken fried rice

ingredients

serves 4

½ tbsp sesame oil

6 shallots, peeled and cut into quarters

450 g/1 lb cooked chicken, cubed

3 tbsp soy sauce

2 carrots, diced

1 celery stick, diced

1 red pepper, deseeded and diced

175 g/6 oz fresh peas

100 g/3½ oz canned sweetcorn, drained

275 g/9¾ oz cooked long-grain rice

2 large eggs

method

1 Heat the oil in a preheated wok or large frying pan over a medium heat.

2 Add the shallots and fry until soft, then add the chicken and 2 tablespoons of the soy sauce and stir-fry for 5–6 minutes.

3 Stir in the carrots, celery, red pepper, peas and sweetcorn and stir-fry for a further 5 minutes. Add the rice and stir thoroughly. Finally, beat the eggs and pour into the mixture. Stir until the eggs are beginning to set, then add in the remaining soy sauce.

risotto with chargrilled chicken breast

ingredients

serves 4

4 boneless chicken breasts,
    about 115 g/4 oz each
salt and pepper
grated rind and juice of 1 lemon
5 tbsp olive oil
1 garlic clove, crushed
8 fresh thyme sprigs,
    finely chopped
3 tbsp butter
1 small onion, finely chopped
280 g/10 oz Arborio rice
150 ml/5 fl oz dry white wine
1 litre/1¾ pints simmering
    chicken stock
85 g/3 oz freshly grated Parmesan
    or Grana Padano cheese
salt and pepper
lemon wedges and fresh thyme
    sprigs, to garnish

method

1 Place the chicken breasts in a shallow dish and season. Mix together the lemon rind and juice, 4 tablespoons of the olive oil, the garlic and thyme. Spoon over the chicken and rub in. Cool, cover and marinate for 4–6 hours, then return to room temperature.

2 Preheat a griddle pan over high heat. Cook the chicken, skin-side down, for 10 minutes, or until the skin is crisp and starting to brown. Turn over and brown the underside. Reduce the heat and cook for 10–15 minutes, or until the juices run clear. Let rest on a carving board for 5 minutes, then cut into thick slices.

3 Meanwhile, melt 2 tablespoons of the butter with the remaining oil in a saucepan over medium heat. Cook the onion, stirring occasionally, until soft and starting to turn golden. Reduce the heat, stir in the rice and cook, stirring, for 2–3 minutes, until translucent. Add the wine and cook, stirring, for 1 minute until reduced. Add the hot stock, a ladleful at a time, stirring constantly, until all the liquid is absorbed and the rice is creamy. Season with salt and pepper. Remove from the heat and stir in the butter and the Parmesan. Serve at once, topped with the chicken slices and garnished with lemon wedges and thyme sprigs.

chicken, mushroom & cashew nut risotto

ingredients

serves 4

55 g/2 oz butter
1 onion, chopped
250 g/9 oz skinless, boneless chicken breasts, diced
350 g/12 oz Arborio rice
1 tsp ground turmeric
150 ml/5 fl oz white wine
1.4 litres/2½ pints simmering chicken stock
75 g/2¾ oz chestnut mushrooms, sliced
50 g/1¾ oz cashews nuts, halved
salt and pepper
wild rocket, fresh Parmesan cheese shavings, and fresh basil leaves, to garnish

method

1 Melt the butter in a large saucepan over medium heat. Add the onion and cook, stirring occasionally, for 5 minutes, or until softened. Add the chicken and cook, stirring frequently, for a further 5 minutes. Reduce the heat, add the rice and mix to coat in butter. Cook, stirring constantly, for 2–3 minutes, or until the grains are translucent. Stir in the turmeric, then add the wine. Cook, stirring constantly, for 1 minute until reduced.

2 Gradually add the hot stock, a ladleful at a time. Stir constantly and add more liquid as the rice absorbs each addition. Increase the heat to medium so that the liquid bubbles. Cook for 20 minutes, or until all the liquid is absorbed and the rice is creamy. About 3 minutes before the end of the cooking time, stir in the mushrooms and cashews. Season with salt and pepper.

3 Arrange the rocket leaves on 4 individual serving plates. Remove the risotto from the heat and spoon it over the rocket. Sprinkle over the Parmesan shavings and basil leaves and serve.

risotto alla milanese

ingredients

serves 4

125 g/4½ oz butter
900 g/2 lb skinless, boneless
    chicken breasts, thinly sliced
1 large onion, chopped
500 g/1 lb 2 oz Arborio rice
150 ml/5 fl oz white wine
1 tsp crushed saffron threads
625 ml/1 pint simmering
    chicken stock
salt and pepper
fresh flat-leaf parsley sprigs,
    to garnish
55 g/2 oz Parmesan cheese
    shavings, to serve

method

1 Melt 55 g/2 oz of the butter in a deep frying pan.
    Add the chicken and onion and cook over medium
    heat, stirring occasionally, for 8–10 minutes, until
    golden brown.

2 Reduce the heat, add the rice and cook, stirring
    constantly, for a few minutes until the grains begin
    to swell and are thoroughly coated in the butter.

3 Add the wine and saffron and season with salt and
    pepper. Cook, stirring constantly, until the wine has
    completely evaporated. Add 2 ladlefuls of the hot
    stock and cook, stirring constantly, until it has been
    completely absorbed. Add the remaining stock,
    1 ladleful at a time, stirring constantly and allowing
    each ladleful to be absorbed before adding the next,
    until all the stock has been absorbed and the rice has
    a creamy texture – this will take 20–25 minutes.

4 Garnish each individual plate with a parsley sprig,
    then serve the risotto immediately, sprinkled with
    the Parmesan cheese shavings and dotted with the
    remaining butter.

chicken basquaise

ingredients

serves 4–5

1 chicken, weighing 1.3 kg/3 lb,
    cut into 8 pieces
flour, for coating
3 tbsp olive oil
1 Spanish onion, thickly sliced
2 red, green or yellow peppers,
    deseeded and cut lengthways
    into thick strips
2 garlic cloves
150 g/5 oz chorizo sausage,
    skinned and cut into 1-cm/
    ½-inch pieces
1 tbsp tomato purée
200 g/7 oz long-grain white rice
450 ml/16 fl oz chicken stock
1 tsp crushed dried chillies
½ tsp dried thyme
115 g/4 oz Bayonne or other
    air-dried ham, diced
12 dry-cured black olives
2 tbsp chopped fresh parsley
salt and pepper

method

1 Pat the chicken pieces dry with kitchen paper. Put
    2 tablespoons of flour in a polythene bag, season
    well with salt and pepper and add the chicken pieces.
    Seal the bag and shake to coat the chicken. Heat
    2 tablespoons of the oil in a large flameproof casserole
    over a medium–high heat. Add the chicken and
    cook, turning frequently, for 15 minutes, or until well
    browned all over. Transfer to a plate.

2 Heat the remaining oil in the casserole and add the
    onion and peppers. Reduce the heat to medium and
    stir-fry until beginning to colour and soften. Add the
    garlic, chorizo and tomato purée and cook, stirring
    constantly, for about 3 minutes. Add the rice and
    cook, stirring to coat, for 2 minutes, or until the rice is
    translucent. Add the stock, crushed chillies and thyme,
    season to taste with salt and pepper and stir well.

3 Bring to the boil. Return the chicken to the casserole,
    pressing it gently into the rice. Cover and cook over
    a very low heat for 45 minutes, or until the chicken is
    cooked through and the rice is tender. Stir the ham,
    black olives and half the parsley into the rice mixture.

4 Re-cover and heat through for a further 5 minutes.
    Sprinkle with the remaining parsley and serve the
    casserole immediately.

chicken & prawn paella

ingredients

serves 6–8

¹/₂ tsp saffron threads

2 tbsp hot water

about 6 tbsp olive oil

6–8 chicken thighs (on the bone, skin on), excess fat removed

140 g/5 oz Spanish chorizo sausage, casing removed, cut into 5-mm/¹/₄-inch slices

2 large onions, chopped

4 large garlic cloves, crushed

1 tsp mild or hot Spanish paprika, to taste

375 g/13 oz medium-grain paella rice

100 g/3¹/₂ oz green beans, chopped

85 g/3 oz frozen peas

1.25 litres/2 pints chicken stock

16 live mussels, scrubbed and debearded (discard any that refuse to close)

16 raw prawns, shelled and deveined

2 red peppers, grilled, peeled, deseeded and sliced

salt and pepper

35 g/1¹/₄ oz fresh parsley, chopped, to garnish

method

1 Put the saffron threads and water in a small bowl and infuse for a few minutes.

2 Heat 3 tablespoons of the oil in a 30-cm/12-inch paella pan. Cook the chicken thighs over medium–high heat, turning frequently, for 5 minutes, or until golden and crispy. Transfer to a bowl. Add the chorizo to the pan and cook, stirring, for 1 minute, or until beginning to crisp. Add to the chicken.

3 Heat another 3 tablespoons of the oil in the pan and cook the onions, stirring frequently, for 2 minutes, then add the garlic and paprika and cook, stirring, for 3 minutes, or until the onions are soft, but not browned. Add the rice, beans and peas and stir until coated in oil. Return the chicken, chorizo and any juices to the pan. Stir in the stock and the saffron with its soaking liquid, and season with salt and pepper. Bring to the boil, stirring constantly, then simmer, uncovered, for 15 minutes, or until the rice is tender and most of the liquid has been absorbed.

4 Arrange the mussels, prawns and red pepper slices on top, then cover and simmer, without stirring, for 5 minutes, or until the prawns turn pink and the mussels open. Discard any mussels that remain closed. Serve at once, sprinkled with the parsley.

sunshine paella

ingredients

serves 4–6

1/2 tsp saffron threads
2 tbsp hot water
150 g/5 1/2 oz cod, rinsed
1.4 litres/2 1/2 pints fish stock
12 large raw prawns, shelled
    and deveined
200 g/7 oz live mussels, scrubbed
    and debearded
3 tbsp olive oil
150 g/5 1/2 oz chicken breast, cut
    into bite-size chunks and
    seasoned to taste
1 large red onion, chopped
2 garlic cloves, chopped
1/2 tsp cayenne pepper
1/2 tsp paprika
225 g/8 oz tomatoes, peeled and
    cut into wedges
1 red pepper and 1 yellow pepper,
    deseeded and sliced
375 g/13 oz paella rice
salt and pepper
175 g/6 oz canned sweetcorn
    kernels, drained
3 hard-boiled eggs, cut into
    quarters lengthways, to serve
lemon wedges, to serve

method

1 Put the saffron threads and water in a bowl and infuse. Cook the cod in the simmering stock for 5 minutes. Rinse, drain, cut into chunks and set aside in a bowl. Cook the prawns in the stock for 2 minutes. Add to the cod. Discard any mussels with broken shells or that refuse to close when tapped. Add to the stock and cook until opened. Add to the bowl with the other seafood, discarding any that remain closed.

2 Heat the oil in a paella pan over medium heat. Cook the chicken, stirring, for 5 minutes. Add the onion and cook, stirring, until softened. Add the garlic, cayenne pepper, paprika and saffron and its soaking liquid and cook, stirring, for 1 minute. Add the tomatoes and peppers and cook, stirring, for 2 minutes.

3 Add the rice and cook, stirring, for 1 minute. Add most of the stock, bring to the boil, then simmer, uncovered, for 10 minutes. Do not stir during cooking, but shake the pan once or twice and when adding ingredients. Season, then cook for 10 minutes, or until the rice is almost cooked, adding more stock if necessary. Add the seafood and corn and cook for 3 minutes.

4 When all the liquid has been absorbed, remove from the heat. Cover with foil and stand for 5 minutes. Serve topped with egg and garnished with lemon wedges.

chicken & duck paella with orange

ingredients

serves 4–6

¹/₂ tsp saffron threads
2 tbsp hot water
175 g/6 oz skinless, boneless
    chicken breast
4 large skinless, boneless
    duck breasts
2 tbsp olive oil
1 large onion, chopped
2 garlic cloves, crushed
1 tsp paprika
225 g/8 oz tomato wedges
1 orange pepper, grilled, peeled,
    deseeded and chopped
175 g/6 oz canned red kidney
    beans (drained weight)
375 g/13 oz paella rice
1 tbsp chopped fresh flat-leaf
    parsley, plus extra sprigs
    to garnish
1 tbsp freshly grated orange rind
2 tbsp orange juice
100 ml/3¹/₂ fl oz white wine
1.25 litres/2 pints simmering
    chicken stock
salt and pepper
orange wedges, to garnish

method

1 Put the saffron threads and water in a small bowl and infuse for a few minutes.

2 Cut the chicken and duck into bite-size chunks and season. Heat the oil in a paella pan and cook the chicken and duck over medium–high heat, stirring, until golden all over. Transfer to a bowl and set aside.

3 Add the onion and cook over medium heat, stirring, until softened. Add the garlic, paprika and saffron and its soaking liquid and cook, stirring constantly, for 1 minute. Add the tomato wedges, orange pepper and beans and cook, stirring, for a further 2 minutes.

4 Add the rice and parsley and cook, stirring, for 1 minute. Add the orange rind and juice, the wine and most of the hot stock. Bring to the boil, then simmer, uncovered, for 10 minutes. Do not stir during cooking, but shake the pan once or twice, and when adding ingredients. Return the chicken and duck to the pan and season. Cook for 10–15 minutes, or until the rice grains are plump and cooked, adding a little more stock if necessary.

5 When all the liquid has been absorbed and you detect a faint toasty aroma coming from the rice, remove from the heat. Cover and stand for 5 minutes. Garnish with parsley sprigs and orange wedges to serve.

paella with pork & chorizo

ingredients

serves 4–6

12 large raw prawns, in their shells
1.25 litres/2 pints simmering
    fish stock
½ tsp saffron threads
2 tbsp hot water
100 g/3½ oz skinless, boneless
    chicken breast, cut into 1-cm/
    ½-inch pieces
100 g/3½ oz pork tenderloin, cut
    into 1-cm/½-inch pieces
3 tbsp olive oil
100 g/3½ oz Spanish chorizo
    sausage, casing removed, cut
    into 1-cm/½-inch slices
1 large red onion, chopped
2 garlic cloves, crushed
½ tsp cayenne pepper
½ tsp paprika
1 red pepper, deseeded
    and sliced
1 green pepper, deseeded
    and sliced
12 cherry tomatoes, halved
375 g/13 oz paella rice
1 tbsp chopped fresh parsley
2 tsp chopped fresh tarragon
salt and pepper

method

1 Add the prawns to the simmering stock and cook for
   2 minutes, then transfer to a bowl and set aside. Put
   the saffron threads and water in a small bowl and
   infuse for a few minutes.

2 Season the chicken and pork with salt and pepper.
   Heat the oil in a paella pan and cook the chicken, pork
   and chorizo over medium heat, stirring, until golden.
   Add the onion and cook, stirring, until softened. Add
   the garlic, cayenne pepper, paprika and saffron and
   its soaking liquid and cook, stirring constantly, for
   1 minute. Add the peppers and tomatoes and cook,
   stirring, for a further 2 minutes.

3 Add the rice and herbs and cook, stirring constantly,
   for 1 minute. Pour in most of the hot stock, bring to
   the boil, then simmer, uncovered, for 10 minutes.
   Do not stir during cooking, but shake the pan once
   or twice and when adding ingredients. Season, then
   cook for a further 10 minutes, or until the rice is almost
   cooked, adding a little more hot stock if necessary.
   Add the prawns and cook for a further 2 minutes.

4 When all the liquid has been absorbed and you detect
   a faint toasty aroma coming from the rice, remove from
   the heat. Cover with foil and stand for 5 minutes. Serve.

greek chicken with rice

ingredients

serves 4

8 chicken thighs
2 tbsp corn oil
1 onion, chopped
2 garlic cloves, finely chopped
175 g/6 oz long-grain rice
225 ml/8 fl oz chicken stock
800 g/1 lb 12 oz canned
    chopped tomatoes
1 tbsp chopped fresh thyme
2 tbsp chopped fresh oregano
12 black olives, pitted and chopped
55 g/2 oz Feta cheese, crumbled
fresh oregano sprigs, to garnish

method

1 Remove the skin from the chicken. Heat the oil in a flameproof casserole. Add the chicken, in batches, if necessary, and cook over medium heat, turning occasionally, for 8–10 minutes, or until golden. Transfer to a plate with a perforated spoon.

2 Add the onion, garlic, rice and 50 ml/2 fl oz of the stock to the casserole and cook, stirring, for 5 minutes, or until the onion is softened. Pour in the remaining stock and add the tomatoes and their juices and the herbs.

3 Return the chicken thighs to the casserole, pushing them down into the rice. Bring to the boil, then reduce the heat, cover and simmer for 25–30 minutes, or until the chicken is cooked through and tender. Stir in the olives and sprinkle the cheese on top. Garnish with oregano sprigs and serve immediately.

jambalaya

ingredients

serves 4

400 g/14 oz skinless, boneless
    chicken breast, diced
1 red onion, diced
1 garlic clove, crushed
625 ml/1 pint chicken stock
400 g/14 oz canned chopped
    tomatoes in tomato juice
280 g/10 oz brown rice
1–2 tsp hot chilli powder
½ tsp paprika
1 tsp dried oregano
1 red pepper, deseeded and diced
1 yellow pepper, deseeded
    and diced
85 g/3 oz frozen sweetcorn kernels
85 g/3 oz frozen peas
3 tbsp chopped fresh parsley
pepper
crisp salad leaves, to serve
    (optional)

method

1 Put the chicken, onion, garlic, stock, tomatoes and
   rice into a large, heavy-based saucepan. Add the chilli
   powder, paprika and oregano and stir well. Bring to
   the boil, then reduce the heat, cover and simmer for
   25 minutes.

2 Add the red and yellow peppers, sweetcorn and peas
   to the rice mixture and return to the boil. Reduce the
   heat, cover and simmer for a further 10 minutes, or
   until the rice is just tender (brown rice retains a 'nutty'
   texture when cooked) and most of the stock has been
   absorbed but is not completely dry.

3 Stir in 2 tablespoons of the parsley and season with
   pepper. Transfer the jambalaya to a warmed serving
   dish, garnish with the remaining parsley, and serve
   with crisp salad leaves, if using.

egg-fried rice with chicken

ingredients

serves 4

225 g/8 oz jasmine rice

3 skinless, boneless chicken breasts, cut into cubes

400 ml/14 fl oz canned coconut milk

50 g/1¾ oz block creamed coconut, chopped

2–3 coriander roots, chopped

thinly pared rind of 1 lemon

1 fresh green chilli, deseeded and chopped

3 fresh Thai basil leaves

1 tbsp Thai fish sauce

1 tbsp oil

3 eggs, beaten

fresh chives and sprigs fresh coriander, to garnish

method

1 Cook the rice in boiling water for 12–15 minutes, drain well, then cool and chill overnight.

2 Put the chicken into a saucepan and cover with the coconut milk. Add the creamed coconut, coriander roots, lemon rind and chilli and bring to the boil. Simmer for 8–10 minutes, until the chicken is tender. Remove from the heat. Stir in the basil and fish sauce.

3 Meanwhile, heat the oil in a wok and stir-fry the rice for 2–3 minutes. Pour in the eggs and stir until they have cooked and mixed with the rice. Line 4 small ovenproof bowls or ramekins with clingfilm and pack with the rice. Turn out carefully onto serving plates and remove the clingfilm. Garnish with long chives and sprigs of coriander. Serve with the chicken.

hainan chicken rice

ingredients

serves 4–6

1 chicken, weighing
     1.5 kg/3 lb 5 oz
55 g/2 oz fresh ginger, smashed
2 garlic cloves, smashed
1 spring onion, tied in a knot
1 tsp salt
2 tbsp vegetable or peanut oil
chilli or soy dipping sauce,
     to serve

rice

2 tbsp vegetable or peanut oil
5 garlic cloves, finely chopped
5 shallots, finely chopped
350 g/12 oz long-grain rice
950 ml/1¾ pints chicken stock
1 tsp salt

method

1 Wash the chicken and dry thoroughly. Stuff the body
  cavity with the ginger, garlic, spring onion and salt.

2 In a large saucepan, bring enough water to the boil
  to submerge the chicken. Place the chicken in the pan,
  breast-side down. Bring the water back to the boil,
  then turn down the heat and simmer, covered, for
  30–40 minutes. Turn the chicken over once.

3 Remove the chicken and wash in running cold water
  for 2 minutes to stop the cooking. Drain, then rub the
  oil into the skin. Set aside.

4 To prepare the rice, heat the oil in a preheated wok.
  Stir-fry the garlic and shallots until fragrant. Add
  the rice and cook for 3 minutes, stirring rapidly.
  Transfer to a large saucepan and add the chicken
  stock and salt. Bring to the boil, then turn down the
  heat and simmer, covered, for 20 minutes. Turn off
  the heat and steam for a further 5–10 minutes, or
  until the rice is perfectly cooked.

5 To serve, chop the chicken horizontally through the
  bone and skin into chunky wedges. Serve with the rice
  and a chilli or soy dipping sauce.

chicken steamed with rice in lotus leaves

ingredients

serves 4–8

450 g/1 lb glutinous rice, soaked in cold water for 2 hours

450 ml/16 fl oz cold water

1 tsp salt

1 tsp vegetable or peanut oil

4 dried lotus leaves, soaked in hot water for 1 hour

filling

100 g/3½ oz raw small prawns, shelled and deveined

5-cm/2-inch piece of fresh ginger

200 g/7 oz lean chicken meat, cut into bite-size strips

2 tsp light soy sauce

55 g/2 oz dried Chinese mushrooms, soaked in warm water for 20 minutes

1 tbsp vegetable or peanut oil, for frying

200 g/7 oz cha siu or pork loin

1 tbsp Shaoxing rice wine

1 tsp dark soy sauce

½ tsp white pepper

1 tsp sugar

method

1 For the filling, steam the prawns for 5 minutes and set aside. Finely grate the ginger, discarding the fibrous parts on the grater and reserving the liquid that drips through. Marinate the chicken in the light soy sauce and ginger juices for at least 20 minutes. Steam for a few minutes in the marinade. Set aside.

2 Drain the rice and place in a saucepan with the water. Bring to the boil, then add the salt and oil. Cover and cook over very low heat for 15 minutes. Divide into 8 portions and set aside. Squeeze out any excess water from the mushrooms, then finely slice, discarding any tough stems. Reserve the soaking water. In a preheated wok or deep saucepan, heat the oil and stir-fry the pork, prawns and mushrooms for 2 minutes. Stir in the Shaoxing, dark soy sauce, pepper and sugar. Add the reserved mushroom soaking water, if necessary.

3 Rinse and dry the lotus leaves. Place a portion of rice in the centre of each and flatten out to form a 10-cm/4-inch square. Top with the pork mixture and some pieces of chicken. Top with another portion of rice, then fold the lotus leaf to form a tight package. Steam for about 15 minutes. Let rest for 5 minutes, then serve.

chicken with vegetables & coriander rice

ingredients

serves 4

2 tbsp vegetable or peanut oil
1 red onion, chopped
2 garlic cloves, chopped
2.5-cm/1-inch piece fresh ginger,
    peeled and chopped
2 skinless, boneless chicken
    breasts, cut into strips
115 g/4 oz white mushrooms
400 g/14 oz canned
    coconut milk
55 g/2 oz sugar snap peas,
    trimmed and halved
    lengthways
2 tbsp soy sauce
1 tbsp fish sauce

rice

1 tbsp vegetable or peanut oil
1 red onion, sliced
350 g/12 oz rice, cooked and cooled
225 g/8 oz pak choi, torn into
    large pieces
handful of fresh coriander, chopped
2 tbsp Thai soy sauce

method

1 Heat the oil in a wok or large frying pan and sauté the onion, garlic and ginger together for 1–2 minutes.

2 Add the chicken and mushrooms and cook over high heat until browned. Add the coconut milk, sugar snap peas and sauces and bring to the boil. Simmer gently for 4–5 minutes until tender.

3 Heat the oil for the rice in a separate wok or large frying pan and cook the onion until softened, but not browned. Add the cooked rice, pak choi and fresh coriander and heat gently until the leaves have wilted and the rice is hot. Sprinkle over the soy sauce and serve immediately with the chicken.

chicken biryani

ingredients

serves 8

1½ tsp finely chopped fresh ginger

1½ tsp crushed fresh garlic

1 tbsp garam masala

1 tsp chilli powder

½ tsp ground turmeric

2 tsp salt

5 green/white cardamom pods, crushed

300 ml/10 fl oz plain yogurt

1.5 kg/3 lb 5 oz chicken, skinned and cut into 8 pieces

150 ml/5 fl oz milk

1 tsp saffron strands

6 tbsp ghee

2 onions, sliced

450 g/1 lb basmati rice

2 cinnamon sticks

4 black peppercorns

1 tsp black cumin seeds

4 fresh green chillies

4 tbsp lemon juice

2–3 tbsp finely chopped fresh coriander leaves

method

1 Blend the ginger, garlic, garam masala, chilli powder, turmeric, half the salt and the cardamoms together in a bowl. Add the yogurt and chicken pieces and mix well. Cover and marinate in the refrigerator for 3 hours.

2 Boil the milk in a small saucepan, pour over the saffron and set aside.

3 Heat the ghee in a large saucepan. Add the onions and cook until golden. Transfer half of the onions and ghee to a bowl and set aside.

4 Place the rice, cinnamon sticks, peppercorns and black cumin seeds in a saucepan of water. Bring to the boil and remove from the heat when the rice is half-cooked. Drain and place in a bowl. Mix with the remaining salt.

5 Chop the chillies and set aside. Add the chicken mixture to the pan containing the onions. Add half each of the chopped green chillies, lemon juice, coriander and saffron milk. Add the rice, then the rest of the ingredients, including the reserved onions and ghee. Cover tightly and cook over low heat for 1 hour. Check that the meat is cooked through; if it is not cooked, return to the heat, and cook for a further 15 minutes. Mix well before serving.

index